The Last Fire-Eater

Walter Lynwood Fleming Lectures in Southern History

THE LAST FIRE-EATER

Roger A. Pryor and the Search for a Southern Identity

WILLIAM A. LINK

Louisiana State University Press
Baton Rouge

Published by Louisiana State University Press
lsupress.org

Manufactured in the United States of America
First printing

Designer: Barbara Neely Bourgoyne
Typeface: Adobe Text Pro
Printer and binder: Integrated Books International (IBI)

Jacket photograph: Roger A. Pryor in the 1850s. Courtesy of the American Civil War Museum, under the management of Virginia Museum of History & Culture (FIC2009.02465).

Cataloging-in-Publication Data are available from the Library of Congress.

ISBN 978-0-8071-7821-8 (cloth: alk. paper)
ISBN 978-0-8071-7894-2 (pdf)
ISBN 978-0-8071-7893-5 (epub)

CONTENTS

The Last Fire-Eater

INTRODUCTION

This book follows the public career of Roger Atkinson Pryor, secessionist, Civil War general, and earnest advocate of postwar sectional reconciliation. During the run-up to the Civil War, Pryor, as a newspaper editor and politician, was an ardent southern rights Democrat and, eventually, secessionist. Subsequently, however, his life involved a series of remakings. Unlike most fire-eaters, Pryor joined the military as a colonel and rose to the rank of brigadier general, yet the brutality of combat undermined his assumptions about honor, manhood, and the value of war. In the decades after the war, he moved from Virginia to New York City, where, in another remaking, he became a celebrity defense attorney. Regrettably, Pryor left no papers to document his private feelings.[1] Yet there is an ample record in newspapers, both his own writings as well as accounts in both the southern and northern press. During the late antebellum years, Pryor became a symbol of the defense of honor to white southerners and of the bullying methods used by disunionists. Journalists North and South followed him avidly.

The story of Roger A. Pryor has already been told. Two biographies chart the details of his life and those of his wife, Sara, who enjoyed a late-blooming career as a popular historian and memoirist.[2] Sara Pryor crafted a narrative about her husband that helped solidify his image.

Whether she "thought a lot of herself," as one account maintained, Sara became one of the most prolific southern white female authors of her generation.[3]

Rather than provide another biography, this book explores the paths of an intriguing figure who was a secessionist, soldier, and reconstructed southern white man. Pryor's journey—and the South's journey—was puzzling and contradictory yet also significant. My intention is to use Pryor as a central, perhaps representative figure during a crucial period in southern history, between the 1850s and the close of the nineteenth century. Pryor remade himself with the changing times. An archetypical southern-rights advocate, he became a skilled practitioner in the politics of honor. Engaging in duels, both attempted and real, he portrayed the world through the cultural prism of southern honor and assumed a more militant and aggressive stance on slavery than his regional peers. Bridging the sectional divide, Pryor adopted the elaborate public staging and ritual associated with the *code duello.* Later, he served prominently in the Civil War. Captured late in the war, he abandoned his fiery persona and renounced fire-eater extremism. Afterward, he moved north to New York City, where he became a prominent lawyer and advocate for intersectional reconciliation.

Pryor lived during a time of great change. The US South changed from an economy dependent on enslaved labor into a region in which racial oppression manifested itself most cruelly in racial violence and Jim Crow segregation. But even more fundamental was a change in the performative nature of manhood and honor—and what it meant to be a man. In particular, values of honor, seemingly fixed in the antebellum South, proved malleable—not fixed but adaptive—during the last half of the nineteenth century. The cataclysmic Civil War, which brought the defeat of the Confederate project and the destruction of slavery, forced a reformulation caused by this revolutionary moment. Pryor thus renounced secession and embraced sectional reconciliation.

Since the publication in 1983 of Bertram Wyatt-Brown's seminal work on southern honor, there has been a profusion of studies about masculinity in the antebellum South. As Stephen Berry writes, men in the region became archetypical "petty tyrants, animated by desires for authority, mastery." Although manly mastery was a trope—the reality of southern manhood may have been different and more complex—the cultural image was one of the "men of the Old South . . . found perched on their self-conceived thrones like great birds atop a promising egg." Southern elite white men served a broader constituency, ruling over their families, free and enslaved, as "patriarchs, men [who] were expected to provide a varied constituency" and acted as "provider, lawgiver, governor, [and] autocrat."[4]

Manliness was a national and not exclusively regional notion, but in the South it was honor based. Honor was both public and private. The honorable public man exhibited manliness through strength, along with self-reliance, individualism and independence, and displaying military prowess. Amy Greenberg describes the diversity of this projected manliness by dividing antebellum masculinity into two competing notions, "restrained manhood" and "martial manhood." While restrained manhood prevailed in the North, many southerners rejected it. "Martial men," Greenberg writes, "believed that the masculine qualities of strength, aggression, and even violence, better defined a true man than did the firm and upright manliness of restrained men." Southern elite whites were quick to anger and exhibited values of patriarchy; these values also dominated, in a different form, the culture of white nonslaveholders. Both groups internalized the "need to maintain honor even at the cost of one's life."[5]

Pryor's reputation as an up-and-coming Democratic partisan during the 1850s reflected his intense ambition as well as his explosive public persona. These characteristics followed standards of political behavior in the South. As Kenneth S. Greenberg writes, public opinion held that elite white southerners like Pryor should never openly seek political office. But in order to win acclaim under the code of honor, they also needed to assert their "superiority and power." Leaders modeled themselves on slaveholder values of mastery and power.[6] Pryor succeeded in attracting attention as a man of honor, hotheaded in political combat but jealous of his standing. Especially in the honor-bound culture of antebellum southerners, appearance and bearing proved all important.

Much of Pryor's public persona involved performance, and observers came away impressed by his stage presence. One contemporary described his "long hair, classic face, dressed in the finest style," and a "fire of genius in his eye" while Pryor spoke with a "clear, well-tuned and penetrating voice."[7] One newspaper commented about his performance at the Southern Commercial Convention that met in September 1857 in Knoxville, Tennessee. "He looks so young as to cause surprise at the distinction he has attained," wrote a newspaperman. Although only twenty-eight years old, "he does not appear to be over twenty-one." Pryor, according to this account, had a "clear, musical voice, the first tone of which attracts attention and commands silence." He had become the "young Hercules of the Convention."[8]

Impressed by his appearance, contemporaries described Pryor's almost feminine traits. Tall, well-dressed, and with long dark hair, he was a striking figure. Accounts often referred to his long hair and the delicacy of his features. One observer said that, beardless, Pryor "could hardly be of the constitutional age"; at a distance "he does not look as if he required a razor to keep his face clean." His long hair hung "behind his ears in the style to which some young ladies now affect."[9] According to one especially detailed account, Pryor was a "slight figure, with a set of features remarkable for their intellectual cast; a profusion of dark hair falling from his brow in long, straight masses over the collar of his coat gave a student-like air to his whole appearance."[10] Another Virginian subsequently remembered that his wife, Sara, was "scared to death" of her husband and used to stand by his chair combing his long hair.[11] A Louisiana reporter said that he "reminded me of a bonnie bit of a woman dressed in a uniform." When he opened his "pretty lips," Pryor still performed like a soldier, though he nonetheless appeared like a "bouncing, spirited girl, trimmed out for war. . . . He walks like one, talks like one, and looks like one when he . . . gives the command of his superiors."[12]

Pryor's oratory was, to many observers, effective. One account described him as having a "tenor voice, a little wiry, and not yet quite trained to the size of the Congressional chamber." He had an "admirable" use of language, while his gestures "possess a most suggestive force." This account described him as "one of the most rising young men in Congress." With his experience as a duelist, he was a "permanent Professor in the College of Honor." Like a doctor ministering to physical ailments, Pryor could "consult on hopeless cases of wounded pride."[13]

The Virginian's bearing further suggested a man with inflammatory qualities that helped project his public persona. In speaking appearances, said one contemporary, Pryor sat on a "vault full of inflammable gas," which was "likely to explode with the first light introduced into it."[14] The metaphor of explosive gas is apt, for his personal appearance added to the power of his rhetoric. A *New York Times* correspondent described Pryor as "sparely and actively built," with a large head that this person described as of the "Emersonian type." His head also suggested "perceptive faculties" that lay "coiled for belligerent and analytical purposes." Noticing his large dark-blue eyes, the correspondent described his "very soft and silky" hair that was "combed back behind his ears and reaching to his coat collar." Pryor had a thin nose that was described as "decisively Grecian, with contracting and dilating nostrils." His mouth was "well arched and sinewy, furnished with two fine, firm rows of teeth—the upper row not lying quite close together, and a little inclined to protrude." Pryor had a chin that was square but "retreating, with a pleasant dimple in its heart." His dress suggested a "scrupulous neatness and nicety of person, encased in a full dress suit of black." Describing Pryor's vocal qualities, this account said that he was a tenor, with a compelling command of language and gestures that, though "very moderate and restrained," offered a "most suggestive force." He was an aggressive speaker, with invectives that were "cool, slow and bitter—giving every arrow time to rankle before the shaft is lodged beside it."[15]

Pryor was a leading exemplar of "Southern Chivalry," honor bound, aggressive, and trigger happy. The sectional debate, as he and other fire-eaters portrayed it, became a larger stage in which political leaders emphasized performance. Their rhetoric sought to defend southern honor against northern aggression. The use of language and performance became a defining characteristic of southern fire-eaters, testing these characteristics even against disunion and war.

During the spring of 1861 at the age of thirty-two, Pryor emerged as a leading secessionist. Like other fire-eaters, his message connected values of disunionism with honor. His strong support for secession drew from and expanded his newspaper celebrity; he became a symbol of younger southerners who denounced compromise. Pryor and others encountered stiff opposition from northerners, especially Republicans, to making any concessions to southern extremism. Impatient with fire-eaters' bluster, Republicans were ready to call their bluff. Such men were "uneasy spirits," products of a slaveocracy and a "vicious social organization," said Washington's *National Republican* in March 1861. Southern demagogues had been "blustering and threatening for twenty years," the newspaper argued, and the time had come to meet extremism with "cold lead and cold steel." Pryor, well known nationally, displayed what it called a "true style of disunion bullying." Now, it said, Americans must respond to "Roger A. Pryor and Roger A. Pryor's associates."[16]

Fire-eater militancy ultimately led to secession and the Civil War, but the reality of brutal warfare undermined their language. The brutalizing experience of battle exposed the emptiness of fire-eater rhetoric. Entering the war as an avid secessionist and warmonger—perhaps more importantly as a representative of the South's culture of honor—Pryor concluded his military participation by renouncing secession and re-creating himself into an advocate of peace and reconciliation.

Recent scholarship emphasizes the effects of war trauma, both physical and psychological, on Civil War soldiers returning home. Clearly, the long-term consequences of horrific combat remain a fertile ground for future scholarly examination.[17] Roger Pryor's wartime experiences provide a lens into how the Civil War affected Confederate soldiers. In his case, the war utterly dispelled his militant masculinity and demonstrated how bluster and hyperbole—the fantasy world that antebellum southern radicalism inhabited—were ill suited to the battlefield.

Pryor had a checkered military career. Despite his efforts to inflate his successes, he was ill prepared to lead men into war. His antebellum definition of honor and manhood was, however, put to the test. Commissioned as a colonel in May 1861, he was promoted to brigadier general by April 1862. Both his commission as colonel and promotion to general reflected his political influence—he also served as a congressman in the Confederate Congress—rather than any military accomplishments. At two key battles, Second Manassas and Antietam, his deficiencies were revealed. Most likely as a result of these deficiencies, he lost his command in September 1862, becoming a general without troops. In August 1863, after months of desk duty, Pryor resigned his commission and reenlisted as a private. Serving as a cavalry scout, he provided intelligence to the Army of Northern Virginia. Late in the war, in November 1864, he was captured after crossing the trench lines at Petersburg. He served about four months in prison at Fort Lafayette in New York harbor. Only through the intervention of newspaper friends, and Pres. Abraham Lincoln's decision to parole him, was he freed.

With Confederate defeat, Pryor renounced his support for secession and urged fellow white southerners to accept defeat. Soon after the war he moved from Virginia to New York City. Trying out newspaper work first, he obtained a law license and began a practice as a defense attorney. While having abandoned the Chivalry, he emphasized personal characteristics and appearance in order to attract public regard. Throughout his life, Pryor was especially successful in attracting newspaper notice. As a contemporary wrote in late 1867, though Pryor had "entirely passed from public view," he had not "lost the power to awaken admiration in the minds of people who like men of his stamp." According to one reporter, he was a "singular mixture, both in form and feature." He was tall, "with a very slight stoop," and in appearance presented himself as a "perfect Apollo." His hair remained a distinguishing feature: "long raven locks" that hung on "drooping shoulders." His face, according to this account, was "illuminated by a pair of eyes that flash at times with the strangest light." Pryor presented a bearing that communicated that he was a "man of mark, so easily can you perceive the fire of genius shining through them from the soul within." No one could "deny the spell of his comeliness."[18]

The Civil War radically altered Pryor's views on honor, politics, and regional identity. Relentless self-promotion during the 1850s had brought him nationwide celebrity. As the Confederacy collapsed, the extremists' pitch for secession rang hollow; flamboyance and bluster meant little on the battlefield. Once the war had ended, Pryor pivoted away from radicalism. Abandoning political extremism, antebellum values no longer guided him. Instead, he proved more flexible and moderate in his self-understanding of the world. In addition, Pryor sought fame in a way that promoted a different version of the meaning of Confederate defeat. His journey led to a complete repudiation of prewar radicalism in favor of political moderation and North-South reconciliation.

In many respects, Pryor's varied career stands out and makes him unique among post–Civil War white southerners. While adopting some elements of the Lost Cause, he publicly renounced secession, slavery, and the Confederacy. Nor was Pryor blissfully optimistic about what others called the New South. Rather, he represented a new adaptation of white southern identity, a leader who fully accepted Yankee ways by adopting them and living in New York for more than a half century. Pryor represented a new sort of white southerner who was no longer obsessed with personal honor, accepted defeat, and even, to a greater extent than was typical, endorsed a modicum of civil rights for freedpeople. His life became an example of a southern exile who shifted his value systems over time and endorsed the changes that the war had brought.

Pryor's change in persona reflected a reconfiguration of the meaning of southern masculinity. Abandoning the bluster and rhetorical excess as well as the militant manhood of the antebellum years, he was now a man of peace and stability. In his public admission of guilt for the Civil War, Pryor did something that few southerners were capable of doing. But the transformation was not just in political outlook. It also meant a reconsideration of manhood and honor, which now became, for him, malleable and situationally adaptable. Circumstances could shape the moment. In order to realize ambition and achieve fame, a man had to act and think with flexibility. Pryor's postwar experience speaks to a version of southern manliness that historians have not fully appreciated.

Roger A. Pryor in the 1850s.
Courtesy of the Virginia Museum of History & Culture, Richmond.

Pryor's shift from fire-eater to soldier and then to attorney is suggestive of the changed circumstances to which he was able to adapt. As a trigger-happy fire-eater, Pryor believed that conflict, especially about personal honor, could be best resolved according to a chivalric code. That code was itself a social construction, but its appeal was widespread in the immediate antebellum years. This changed fundamentally with the conclusion of the Civil War. Not only did the war evoke a "crisis in gender," as LeeAnn Whites aptly puts it, but also occasioned the transformation of attitudes among southern whites of Pryor's class about the resolution of personal conflict. Duels were no longer popular and, in general, no longer tolerated by public opinion. With the end of the war, the law became the main arena for individuals to combat each other.[19]

In striking contrast to his 1850s persona, the Roger Pryor of the postwar period became an advocate for sectional reconciliation. Soon after the war he urged fellow white southerners to accept the end of slavery. By the 1870s, he told southern and northern veterans to seek reconciliation and to bind the wounds of war. In 1880, a New Yorker described Pryor as a leading advocate of reconciliation between North and South in the Civil War's aftermath. After Confederate defeat he was "one of the first to accept the situation with grace and dignity." Because of his determination to accept defeat, he "won the respect and confidence . . . of all his fellow citizens." As part of his professional and political success, the post–Civil War Pryor became a leading voice for intersectional reconciliation.[20]

Pryor's speechmaking provided a warmup for his future efforts to promote sectional reconciliation. His approach to sectional reunion meant starkly different rhetoric; rather than a provocateur, he became an ambassador for peace. Behind his new rhetoric was a different attitude toward manliness that was more pragmatic and flexible and less subject to impulsiveness and anger. Pryor, now a leading attorney in a world in which the law rather than duels resolved conflict, became a spokesman for a different version of masculinity; sectional reconciliation became a part of that same transformation. Although he was able to project himself in this manner because he lived in the North, not the South, Pryor nonetheless became an example of a new sort of southern man.

During the early decades of the twentieth century, Pryor encouraged the newspapers' tendencies to lionize his accomplishments in healing the wounds of war. In 1906, the *New York Times* published a long profile that portrayed him as a reconciliationist. The story recounted how, when a group of Yankee veterans invited Pryor to speak on Lincoln's birthday, he declined but instead addressed the group in writing. "Under the guidance of an overruling Providence," he declared, "we who upheld the cause of the Southern Confederacy" also acquiesced in ending slavery and what he called the "consolidation of the Union." The *Times* wondered if Pryor's letter, now made public, would become his "final expression" about the Civil War's aftermath. His message sought out not just veterans. Rather, his conception of sectional reconciliation would "abide in public memory as an eloquent and patriotic valediction." Pryor's statement would be a "renewed token" of how the back and forth of the "political whirligig" turned heated rhetoric "to blessings and benedictions on the road."[21]

Roger Pryor's lifetime encompassed dizzying changes. Born during the administration of John Quincy Adams, he died during the latter days of the presidency of Woodrow Wilson, four months after the end of World War I. He witnessed fundamental transformations in the South with the destruction of slavery and the defeat of the Confederacy. White southerners, as a result of defeat, redefined manhood and honor in such a way that extralegal reliance on honor among white men was no longer resolved by dueling and personal violence.

1

A CHAMPION OF THE SOUTH

On April 5, 1860, forty-nine-year-old Owen Lovejoy, a minister, abolitionist, and Illinois congressman, rose to speak in the US House of Representatives. He condemned the twin relics of barbarism: Mormon polygamy and African American slavery. If every crime in society were put into a "moral crucible," Lovejoy informed his fellow representatives, nothing could outdo the barbarity of slavery. It possessed the "violence of robbery, the blood and cruelty of piracy, and the offensive and brutal lusts of polygamy, all combined and concentrated in itself, with aggravations that neither one of these crimes ever knew or dreamed of." The nation could no longer be both slave and free, Lovejoy believed.

During his speech, the Republican Lovejoy wandered toward the Democratic side of the House chamber, vigorously gesticulating, pointing in the direction of those members, and employing what one observer said was a "loud and denunciatory" manner. Springing to his feet, Virginian Roger Atkinson Pryor moved toward Lovejoy and ordered him to proceed no further. It was bad enough that Pryor was forced to listen to his "treasonable and insulting language," but Lovejoy should not trespass on the Democratic side of the chamber. The House, which had experienced frequent episodes of violence inside the Capitol during the antebellum era, appeared ready to erupt into a melee when fellow Republican John F. Potter of Wisconsin intervened, defending Lovejoy's right of free speech. Republicans had been forced to endure "violent and offensive" attacks for eight weeks, Potter said. "We listened to them quietly, and heard them through," he added. "And now, sir, this side shall be heard, let the consequences be what they may." The House then erupted into mass confusion, as forty members left their seats prepared to fight.[1]

Although order was eventually restored, several days later Pryor visited the congressional printing office to review the report of House proceedings before they appeared in the *Congressional Globe*. Discovering that Potter had amended the proceedings, he deleted these changes. Potter, catching wind of Pryor's intervention, returned and restored his editorial changes, and the *Globe* published his version intact. Now Pryor focused his grievance on Potter rather than Lovejoy. On April 11, 1860, almost a week after the initial incident in the chamber, Pryor announced before the House that Potter had fabricated the disputed portions of the *Globe*'s transcript in order to exaggerate his role. The Wisconsin representative responded that he had simply invoked the privilege of House members to review and edit their remarks. Pryor had no right to "alter a single word or a comma" without consulting him, he maintained. Although Potter's changes were minimal, the Virginian claimed that they were "unwarrantable and impertinent" as well as an affront to his personal honor. Ominously, he warned that he would "put what construction I please upon it," the consequences be damned.[2]

By the Civil War's outbreak, Pryor had become a nationally known fire-eater, a term that gained prominence during the 1850s. Fire-eaters in circus carnivals not only appeared to swallow fire but also entertained the audience with audacious language. In the decade prior to secession, southern politicians who became known as "fire-eaters" were aggressive exponents of what northerners called the "Southern Chivalry." At the heart of the Chivalry was an exaltation of personal honor and an attendant need to protect the values of an honor-based society against perceived external aggression. Honor, as Kenneth Greenberg writes, served as a "vitally important language" that transcended regional and class differences among southern whites.[3] For Pryor and the Chivalry that he exemplified, the personal became political through the *code duello* and the elaborate public stagings and rituals associated with it.

Recent scholarship ties conceptions of masculinity to this rhetoric. Americans shared, as James J. Broomall writes, "well-developed notions of manliness" that "signaled qualities such as strength and fortitude, and located identities in work and family." Fire-eaters' dramatic rhetorical exaggerations resonated differently among northern and southern audiences. Masculinity, in other words, varied regionally. In general, southerners, especially elite southerners, protected a patriarchal family that included control and mastery. While northern whites exalted domesticity and valued what Amy Greenberg calls "restrained" manhood, public behavior required, according to Broomall, "cultivated masks that maintained rigid gender and racial hierarchies."[4] As Reid Mitchell points out, abolitionists considered honor-bound southern culture as unmanly and excessive. Sexual dominance over enslaved women imperiled domestic order, while physical violence represented a false masculinity; "true manhood," writes Mitchell about northerners, "required self-discipline and civilized morality." They considered southern values and their attitudes toward manhood abhorrent.[5]

By April 1860, when he battled with Republicans on the House floor, Pryor had become a hero to white southerners and a villain to northerners. While southern newspapers valorized him, northern publications, especially the Republican press, portrayed him as a deranged and dark specimen of Southern Chivalry—an arrogant and overbearing bully who relied on violence and intimidation. Pryor's reputation as a fire-eater reflected his newspaper celebrity, and over the years newspapers continued to report about him.

Born on July 19, 1828, Pryor was the son of Lucy Atkinson and Presbyterian minister Theodorick Pryor. He grew up in Nottoway County, west of Petersburg, Virginia. After an academy education, he entered Hampden-Sydney College in 1843, graduating as valedictorian in 1845.

Enrolling as a law student at the University of Virginia, Pryor received his degree in 1847. While in Charlottesville, he fell in love with Sara Agnes Rice, and they married on November 8, 1848, when he was twenty and she was eighteen. Admitted to the bar, Pryor opened a law office in Charlottesville but, within two years, developed a serious throat illness and, during his recovery, became a journalist. Acquiring the *Petersburg South-Side Democrat* at age twenty-two, he gained a reputation for political combativeness that emerged in subsequent positions at the *Richmond Enquirer* and the *Richmond South.*

In 1852, when only twenty-two years old, Pryor attended the Democratic National Convention in Baltimore as a delegate from Virginia. Elected as the Virginians' secretary, he and his fellow delegates initially supported Pennsylvanian James Buchanan's presidential bid.[6] Although Michigan's Lewis Cass, the 1848 Democratic presidential nominee, commanded a majority, he fell short of the necessary two-thirds majority, with remaining votes going to Illinois's Stephen A. Douglas or Buchanan. Before the convention's forty-fifth ballot, the Virginia delegation abandoned Buchanan and offered to nominate former US senator Daniel S. Dickinson of New York, but he declined the nomination. In search of an alternative, the Virginians then proposed New Hampshire's Franklin Pierce, who became the Democratic nominee and was subsequently elected president.[7]

Pryor derived considerable political benefit from Pierce's nomination. In September 1852, one newspaper described Pryor as "one of the ablest political writers in the southern states."[8] His standing grew among the regional and national network of Democratic editors, which brought him to the attention of Pierce supporters. Interested in strengthening ties with southerners, Democratic leaders recruited Pryor to help edit the pro-Pierce *Washington Union.*[9] Attracted by the *Union*'s larger salary and the national stage, he sold the *South-Side Democrat* and moved his family to Washington.[10]

In May 1853, only months after he started work at the *Washington Union,* Pryor published a review of Maryland Whig Henry Winter Davis's *The War of Ormuzd and Ahriman.* In this book, Davis, maintaining that the United States and Russia were on a collision course, offered the two as versions of a modern democratic and an autocratic state, respectively. Disagreeing with Davis, Pryor asserted that, though the two countries operated on "antagonist principles," their relations were of the "most amicable kind."[11] Pryor perhaps admired Russia's aristocratic society because it resembled the South's autocratic social and political structure. In Russia, he pointed out, there was none of the "unknown disease" of the "maudlin, mock philanthropy" of Harriet Beecher Stowe's *Uncle Tom's Cabin,* the runaway bestseller that appeared a year earlier in 1852.[12]

In views that reflected his lifelong Anglophobia, Pryor urged closer relations with Russia. "In every element of national strength and happiness," he asserted, Russia was "great and prosperous beyond any other country in Europe." Whig newspapers immediately responded. Pryor's "notorious eulogy on Russia and her despotic Government," observed the *New York Daily Tribune,* constituted a "gratuitous panegyric" and a "preposterous laudation of the Czar." His views were "composed of false reasoning, based on false or at least superficial facts, and resulting in absurd conclusions," asserted the *Tribune.* Pryor argued for a "complete identity in the interests of Russia and the United States" and that a "pure and eternal friendship" was "their joint destiny."[13]

This essay stirred up opposition from both Whigs and Democrats. There were "many amusing evidences of the zeal with which our Democratic contemporaries hasten to purge themselves of all responsibility for the "Russian article," noted the *Washington Republic.* "Why take the side of the most arbitrary, stupid, and stagnant kingdom in the vast realm of Fog[e]ydom? Is it a crime to 'incite the people to revolt'?"[14] Even more seriously, the Pierce administration had tilted toward Britain in its conflict with Russia, which, in October 1853, finally exploded into the Crimean War.

The upshot of the controversy was that Pryor was forced to resign as the *Washington Union*'s coeditor, though Pierce, as a stopgap, appointed him as a special emissary to Greece. In part, this was a patronage appointment, but Pryor was sent with a specific purpose: to resolve the dispute between an American missionary, Jonas King, and the Greek government. King had spent two decades as a Protestant evangelist in Orthodox Christian Greece, and now its government had confiscated some of his properties in Athens. He disputed the seizure, and eventually the Greek authorities decided to negotiate with the US government. Pryor, who left Sara behind in Washington in July 1855 and boarded the liner *Pacific,* visited London and Paris en route, eventually arriving in Athens in October.

Pryor's mission was ultimately successful, though only after further negotiations. The Crimean War was still raging, with French and British forces using Greece as a staging ground for their operations against Russia. Because the Virginian had taken Russia's side during the war, the Greeks—who also sided with Russia—were more favorably disposed toward the new emissary. In addition, the government and its population resented the Anglo-French occupation and now sought American favor. These factors probably figured importantly, perhaps more so than any diplomatic skills on Pryor's part. With intercession by the Russian ambassador, the dispute over King's property was settled in November 1855 in the missionary's favor. After a return trip that featured further stops in Italy, France, and England, Pryor, on the heels of his successful diplomatic intervention, returned to the United States in early 1856.[15] Sara later described her husband's mission to Greece as yet another demonstration of his persuasive powers. As she wrote, he "accomplished the object of his mission to the satisfaction of his government, and to his own pleasure and profit." Roger returned to Virginia with "many beautiful pictures and carvings for the home we now made in Richmond, to say nothing of corals, amber, mosaics, curios, and antiques, silks, laces, velvets, perfumes, etc., to my great content."[16] Although President Pierce offered him an ambassadorship to Persia, Pryor declined the offer and returned to Richmond.

During the summer of 1853, Pryor joined the *Richmond Enquirer,* Virginia's flagship Democratic newspaper.[17] He remained involved in the *Enquirer* until February 1857, when he founded a new newspaper, the *Richmond South.*[18] Sara chose the *South*'s motto—*Unum et commune periculum una salus* (one common peril, one safety). Pryor's tendency

Henry A. Wise.
Library of Congress, Washington, DC.

to seek out controversy fueled his meteoric rise as a newspaper editor and Democratic partisan. According to another observer, it proved impossible for him "not to drift into politics outside of the sanctum of his paper." Soon the Virginia public and a national audience recognized him as an able and eloquent public speaker who joined what his wife diplomatically called the "bitter discussions" of the 1850s.[19]

Pryor experienced political combat during that tumultuous decade, when politics and personal honor were rarely separated. In late September 1852, during that year's presidential campaign, the mercurial former congressman and future governor Henry A. Wise engaged in a debate with Whig William C. Carrington before an audience in Portsmouth, New Hampshire, on behalf of Democratic presidential candidate Pierce. An accomplished speaker who delivered a twenty-five-hour, five-day speech during Virginia's constitutional convention of April 1851, Wise already had a long career as one of his state's preeminent defenders of the code of honor. The Wise-Carrington debate, which began at 7 P.M., proceeded according to prevailing custom: Wise spoke for an hour and a half, as did Carrington afterward. When Wise rejoined for an hour, Carrington was provided equal time. But a disagreement arose when Wise rose to speak for another hour—this after five full hours of debate, the time now past midnight. Before he had the chance to begin anew, the president of the local Whig Chippewa Club, James G. Holliday, complained that the Virginian was violating the accepted rules of debate, which dictated that the discussion had ended. Objecting to that limitation, Wise demanded that the question be put to the audience. Tempers then flared. When Holliday interrupted him in a "tone and manner of surprise," Wise indignantly demanded treatment as a gentleman. Holliday responded that Wise was "false" in inferring unfair treatment. The Virginian immediately responded by striking him in the face, an act designed to be demeaning and humiliating. Although the incident could have easily escalated into violence, the two men were separated and peace restored. Holliday left satisfied, as the newspaper account put it, that this was "an accidental and momentary cause of assault."[20]

Wise's insistence on honor provided a model for his son, O. Jennings "Obie" Wise. He was a political provocateur among other hotheaded colleagues at the *Enquirer.* Obie was also one whom the famous diarist and agricultural reformer Edmund Ruffin called a "professional duelist," a "professional bully for political gain," and a "murderer in intention, if not yet in deed."[21] At a Fourth of July celebration in 1851 in Drummondstown on the Eastern Shore, the ritualized toasts for the occasion got out of control. When a participant ridiculed the Compromise of 1850's "Texas bribe" (in which a large portion of slaveholding western Texas was transferred to the nonslaveholding New Mexico Territory), Eastern Shore congressman Thomas M. Bayly took offense. Intervening, Obie, only twenty years old, announced his willingness to "take my just proportion" of responsibility for the toast, while Bayly informed him that it was "none of your business, Sir." Wise, offended at the congressman's aggressive tone, responded: "I make it my business, Sir. . . . I backed that toast; but I will not back from you. . . . I will *face* you, when and where you dare." Obie then pressed on, determined to force a confrontation. In response, Bayly retreated, saying that he had not used "any offensive language this evening." Wise then pushed the matter even further, describing Bayly as his "father's enemy . . . a coward and a scoundrel." When others asked Obie to leave the room, he confronted the congressman and goaded him with further insults. Bayly refused to take the bait, claiming that Wise's young age barred him from accepting his challenge.[22]

Obie was especially sensitive to any attacks on his father. After Henry Wise was elected governor in 1855, *Richmond Whig* editor Robert Ridgway published regular Whig and Know-Nothing partisan attacks against him.[23] In January 1858, after Ridgway published an editorial highly critical of his father, Obie visited the *Whig*'s offices. There he found Ridgway alone. Announcing that the editor's insolence had become "insupportable," Wise, using his walking stick as a weapon, struck him on his shoulder and dragged him to the middle of the room, where he administered further blows to the head, back, and shoulders. Claiming that Obie was drunk, Ridgway denounced the young man's version of

O. Jennings Wise.

Courtesy of the Indiana University Archives, South Bend.

events as "palpable falsehoods." After the editor responded with the unorthodox suggestion that the two men meet in his office with two pistols, one loaded, one unloaded and dispensed to each other by lot, Wise rejected the challenge, believing that shooting an unarmed man was "entirely incompatible" with the code of honor. As his use of the cane suggested, he considered Ridgway a social inferior with little comprehension of any "just sense of honor and propriety recognised by established usage." Further violence was averted.[24]

Obie's best-known duel occurred in September 1858 and involved Sherrard Clemens, a Wheeling congressman from generally antislavery western Virginia. After John W. Brockenbrough of Augusta County emerged as a possible Democratic contender for the governor's race of 1859, Clemens joined other Democratic congressmen in endorsing Lexington newspaper editor and fellow congressman John Letcher. Clemens published comments stating that Brockenbrough had renounced his intention to run. When Brockenbrough denied this, Obie Wise attacked Clemens in the *Enquirer* in what former congressman John Y. Mason characterized as an "intemperate editorial." After a printed exchange, Clemens challenged Wise to a duel; Pryor agreed to serve as the editor's second. On September 17, 1858, the duelists met at the Fairfield racetrack in Henrico County outside Richmond. Both men missed their first shots, after which Pryor proposed an amicable end to the duel. But when Obie would not apologize, Clemens refused to withdraw his challenge. Two more volleys followed, with both men missing; further negotiations failed. Although Clemens's second threatened to leave, the duel continued. During the fourth volley, Clemens was seriously injured by a bullet to the thigh bone. Wise then left the field unharmed.[25]

As Bertram Wyatt-Brown observes, the relationship between dueling and politics involved "translating personal fury into corporate resentment" while at the same time personalizing political combat. The southern code of honor, writes Wyatt-Brown, was that "cluster of ethical rules, most readily found in societies of small communities, by which judgments of behavior are ratified by community consensus."

Honor involved values of loyalty, manhood, and individual integrity; it infused all ranks of southern society but represented an aristocratic ideal rooted in slave society.[26] Transgressions upon honor could lead to violent resolution, especially with the political environment highly charged during the 1850s and the nature of partisanship explosive. An honor-based social system reflected the hierarchies and values of the slavery regime; it was the political equivalent of paternalism in the master-slave relationship. Yet the social basis of honor eroded during the late antebellum years, and within a generation, honor-based politics gave way to new political forms. While public political behavior was male, there was, as Elizabeth Varon has recently shown, also a private political culture in which women figured prominently. Women frequently appeared in public assemblies and packed the galleries of the legislatures and the major political conventions. And, increasingly, they became ardent advocates of Virginian—and southern—values. For men, transgressions on matters of honor were serious matters indeed, and duels remained a popular means of resolving conflict throughout the 1850s, despite efforts to criminalize them.[27]

Like Obie Wise, Pryor adopted a combative newspaper style that could result in violent consequences. Between 1854 and 1860, he became involved in at least eight attempted or realized duels. His pastor father disapproved, commenting to a contemporary that his son's dueling "disposition . . . had given him great trouble."[28] Dueling revealed the divide between restrained and martial manhood, and a tug-of-war prevailed in the antebellum South between efforts to criminalize the practice and the public's obsession with it.[29] Dueling also exemplified sharp regional differences. The *Wellsburg Herald,* one of the few Republican newspapers in Virginia, was located in a town along the Ohio River in Virginia's western panhandle. The newspaper shared the values of northerners, who increasingly ridiculed dueling. In May 1859, the *Herald* mocked the practice by describing, in racist fashion, a duel that occurred between two Black men. What could be more ludicrous, in the racist imagination of western Virginians, than an affair of honor among Black people, who had no honor? In an incident that may or may not have occurred, two Black men argued about a woman. The duelists, Jack McNutt and Pete Wilson, did not follow the *code duello*. Instead, they mimicked the white culture of honor, but, in a violation of the code, McNutt delivered the challenge himself rather than using a second. "Though deficient in form," the newspaper account continued, "the challenge nevertheless possessed sufficient vital power to inflame the spark of honor in the dusky bosom of Pete." Neither man had experience with firearms, and during the first three rounds, the pistols were accidentally discharged. The scene, concluded the *Herald*, was "awfully ludicrous, and notwithstanding the solemnity of the occasion, the laugh that arose might have been heard a mile." According to the paper, the moral of the story was clear: the duel between Jack and Pete mocked the "barbarous practice of dueling" and brought the "murderous code of the duello into disrepute more than would ten columns of preaching on the immorality of dueling."[30]

Although dueling was criminalized in Virginia through legislation after 1810, its practice peaked during the 1850s.[31] Antidueling provisions were incorporated into the state constitutional revisions of 1830 and 1851, but enforcement was often weak. Although the law could disfranchise duelists, constitutional revisions and laws provided amnesty. Even opponents conceded that dueling would not end until public opinion turned against it. The practice became a marker not only of North-South differences but also, in Virginia, of the gap between East and West. With a smaller enslaved and slaveholder population in western Virginia, the culture of honor was less pronounced, and antidueling sentiment prevailed. The remedy for the law's ineffectiveness, said legislator William Smith of mountainous Greenbrier County, lay in public opinion. Anyone refusing a challenge was "denounced as a coward . . . and a poltroon." He continued: "Let the man who has the moral courage and fortitude to refuse a duel receive the public approbation," and dueling would end. It was futile to discuss enforcing antidueling laws "unless that penal enactment is approved by the deliberate judgment of the people."[32]

As indicators of public opinion, newspapers fed a southern audience hungry for news about affairs of honor. Duelists placed correspondence about challenges and negotiations in the partisan press, which expanded rapidly in Virginia towns and cities after the invention of the steam press during the 1830s. With public scrutiny focusing on duels, newspapers became essential as a venue. Insults exposed southern statesmen to public scrutiny that required a restitution of standing, though dueling only infrequently led to a fight to the death. Despite the ritual lead-up to duels—challenges, the naming of seconds, and the negotiations between the principals—most of these conflicts led to peaceful resolution. As one contemporary wrote, challenges "frequently occurred," but seconds were often able to resolve the disputes through a "reasonable consideration of the difficulty."[33] Dueling often involved intricate negotiations about the choice of weapons and locale, with the seconds brokering these discussions. Public posturing was part of this ritual, with the correspondence documenting the negotiations frequently appearing in newspapers. Local authorities also read newspapers, so duelists played a cat-and-mouse game in balancing public exposure with concern about law enforcement.

During the mid-1850s, the rise of Know-Nothingism seemed to pose a genuine threat to Democratic supremacy in Virginia.[34] During the state's 1855 gubernatorial election, Democratic newspapers portrayed Know-Nothings as only weak protectors of the slavery regime. At the height of the campaign, when Democrat Henry Wise faced Know-Nothing and Whig Thomas Flournoy, *Richmond Whig* editor William S. Easley took offense at a Pryor editorial and challenged him to a duel. Before anything could occur, however, both men were arrested, which effectively ended the possibility of violence.[35] About a year later Pryor challenged Robert Ridgway, Easley's successor as *Richmond Whig* editor.[36] In a public letter he declared that Ridgway's "coarse criticism and offensive insinuation" had crossed a line. Ridgway had chosen to "skulk among verbal ambiguities," and Pryor was obliged to "hold him up to the world as a wilful falsifier, vulgar blackguard, and drunken bully." In this dispute, the terms of the argument shifted from political to personal conflict. Ridgway, Pryor charged, had created a "personal difficulty" that compelled him "to fight him or to degrade me in the esteem of all honorable men."[37]

Pryor and Ridgway agreed to meet outside Washington, DC, but, because the details of the duel were leaked to the press, Richmond and Washington police remained on high alert. The two men met at the Bladensburg dueling grounds, located in Maryland northeast of the District of Columbia. A popular location for duelists, the grounds were situated on the Baltimore-Washington stagecoach road near a small spit of land on a creek that fed into the Anacostia River. What made these dueling grounds so popular was their remoteness, being outside the district, and also isolated enough to evade Maryland authorities. Between 1808 and 1861, the Bladensburg dueling grounds served as a location for about fifty duels, including the famous 1820 Stephen Decatur–James Barrow duel, which resulted in Decatur's death, and the 1830 Jonathan Cilley–William J. Graves duel, which resulted in Cilley's death. On August 8, 1856, the Pryor-Ridgway duel, in the end, amounted to nothing after both men missed their first shot. Ridgway then demanded a second shot, but by then three onlookers had appeared on the scene, one of whom was Preston Brooks, himself a duelist and who had, less than three months earlier, brutally caned Sen. Charles Sumner of Massachusetts. Brooks and his party urged conciliation, and before the pistols could be loaded for a second shot, they achieved an "amicable settlement."[38]

The Ridgway duel illustrates a pattern in which conflicts over personal honor flowed from Pryor's aggressive journalistic and political style but ultimately led to nothing. This was probably because Pryor used aggressive language in public but, in the end, was usually bluffing. More important for him than a duel was the stage of honor, trumpeted by newspaper accounts that could enhance his standing through appeals to honor and masculinity.[39] Fire-eaters' belligerence was more bark than bite, and northern audiences were not buying their rhetoric. Referring to South Carolinian Lawrence Keitt in terms that easily could also describe Pryor, the *Chicago Tribune* described fire-eaters

Charles James Faulkner.
Library of Congress, Washington, DC.

as "habitually overbearing" and exhibiting a "vulgar vanity" that made secessionists believe that they were "the impersonation of Southern Chivalry."[40]

It was not unusual for participants to evade duels without appearing cowardly, in order to attract public attention in the performative rituals of the *code duello without risking violence.* During the 1850s, Whig Alexander R. Boteler and Democrat Charles James Faulkner, longstanding rivals in the northern Shenandoah Valley counties of Berkeley and Jefferson, twice ran against each other for Congress. In 1855, Boteler charged that Faulkner had anonymously written a newspaper account four years before about Henry Bedinger, who challenged Faulkner for Congress in 1851. The newspaper account proved decidedly favorable to Faulkner, a ruthless opportunist, and Boteler possessed an original manuscript of the article establishing Faulkner's authorship. Faulkner took offense and, in August 1855, denounced Boteler, describing his "characteristic weakness and vanity," claiming that he lacked "manly and refined chivalry," and charging him with "equivocating and disgusting conduct." Faulkner concluded by inviting Boteler to seek "honorable redress."[41]

Boteler traveled to Washington with a second, David H. Strother, to deliver a challenge. When they arrived at the Willard Hotel on August 16, 1855, Faulkner declared that his second would accept the challenge, but that man never appeared. Instead, district authorities—tipped off by Faulkner—arrived and arrested Boteler. Faulkner, whom a Boteler supporter described as a "low blackguard traitor & liar," scrupulously avoided receiving the challenge. Meanwhile, during September 1855, he began circulating rumors that Boteler had retreated from this conflict. Negotiations dragged on, and Boteler concluded things discreetly by reaching an "honourable adjustment." He acknowledged that Faulkner was not the author of the anti-Bedinger article on October 8, 1851, while Faulkner admitted that Boteler had made no improper use of the materials nor made unwarranted aspersions on his character.[42]

So ended the episode, which displayed the extent to which partisan politics was enmeshed in the rituals of political culture and traditions of honor. The Boteler-Faulkner encounter of 1855 also illustrated how the code of honor had declined. Boteler accepted the rules of politics and honor; Faulkner, an opportunist and rogue, manipulated that code. "After all, my friend, we have not been hunting a lion, but a fox," Strother, who was Boteler's second, affirmed the conclusion of the episode. "We've holed him indeed," he wrote, "but it's nothing to brag of." The primary motive in any duel, Strother believed, was to "maintain that reputation for courage, manliness & honour which wins the respect of friends, enforces that of one's enemies, & above all secures that self respect without which no high toned man can live or cares to live." On this score, public opinion was "remorseless in its criticisms & requirements."[43]

Like Faulkner, Pryor was mostly bluster, and his conflicts over honor were meant to inflate his importance in public opinion. In March 1855, he wrote an editorial in the *Richmond Enquirer* attacking former Virginia governor William "Extra Billy" Smith, who waded into Democratic Party politics and criticized the convention that had nominated Henry Wise as their candidate for governor in 1855. Pryor asserted that Smith himself benefited from the convention system. "With an air of mingled penitence and pride," Pryor wrote, "he pompously recites his service to the party, and claims impunity for his present misconduct." He further charged that Smith's loyalty to the Democracy was a "calculation of personal interest" rather than an "unselfish support of certain principles of public policy."[44] Months later news of this verbal attack reached Smith's son, Caleb Smith, who lived in California. When he claimed that Pryor's newspaper attack impugned his father's personal honor, Pryor used an evasive response to escape the consequences. He began by denying that his article was anything but a "legitimate criticism" of a public figure, then denied that there was any insult to William Smith's personal honor. Pryor concluded his response by asserting that he would only accept a challenge from the ex-governor himself, not from his son. Moreover, he claimed that, because of his own reputation as a duelist, he was "under bonds to keep the peace" and would incur a "heavy penalty" if he became involved in a duel. Caleb responded that Pryor had written his piece in a "false, malign and vindictive spirit." Moreover, his father was "aged" and too infirm to engage in a duel—this despite the fact that Extra Billy survived the Civil War and lived another three decades.[45]

Pryor's newspaper attacks became a prominent feature of his journalistic style, but as with the Smith incident, he sometimes avoided the prospect of a duel. In 1856, he took on John Minor Botts, a Richmond state senator and three-term Whig congressman. From his perch in Richmond, which was known as the "Gibraltar" of Virginia Whiggery, Botts expressed unconventional ideas that challenged fire-eater orthodoxy. The Democratic press derisively referred to Botts, who had a massive head and body, as "the Bison." Although he was unable to win election during the 1850s, he became a gadfly and also a target for southern radicals. In early October 1856, after Pryor composed an anti-Botts editorial, his son, Beverly B. Botts, published a message in Richmond newspapers suggesting a duel. Pryor responded with a formal challenge, leaving it to the younger Botts to determine the choice of time, place, and weapons. Complicated negotiations followed. Botts demanded that the duel occur not in Richmond, but near Washington; Pryor insisted on Richmond. The difficulty of these negotiations reflected the editor's bombast about honor combined with, most likely, his reluctance to duel. In addition, the more either Botts or Pryor delayed, the more likely it was that Richmond or Washington police might intervene preemptively. Further, the younger Botts suffered from bad health and was ill suited for dueling—one account claimed that he was "so ill as hardly to be able to stand up"—and his delaying tactics might have also indicated that he wanted a way out.[46]

After agreement on terms, more delay followed.[47] While Botts and Pryor dithered, the police were hot on the trail. Earlier, on October 5, Richmond authorities obtained a warrant to arrest both men but failed to locate either. Meanwhile, Richmond and Washington newspapers closely reported the affair and informed the public that the duel was planned for Washington on October 8.[48] Richmond police coordinated with their district counterparts by telegraph, and officers from both cities watched possible locations. In the end, police knew ahead of time that the duel would occur outside Silver Spring, Maryland, near the estate of journalist and politician Francis Preston Blair. Four officers—one from Richmond and three from Washington—moved into action about 4 A.M. on the eighth.[49] When Botts's and Pryor's parties arrived, they and their seconds were arrested and brought before a judge, who released them. Subsequently, a Richmond court declined to prosecute either man.[50]

That did not end matters, however. Frustrated in his attempt to engage Beverly Botts, Pryor on October 12 wrote to his intended target, John Botts. He made the specious claim that he was reluctant to fight Beverly because Pryor possessed proof that the elder Botts had "put him forward" to deliver "insults which you had no excuse to shift to the shoulders of another." When Pryor insisted on a duel, Botts's response must have been startling. He emphatically denounced "any authority" for the assertion that he had encouraged his son to fight a duel. Any fault lay with Pryor, whose life "could not be the value of a pig's pound to me." Still, he had little desire to make Pryor's children fatherless, he wrote. If Botts indulged in false chivalry, he would open himself up to more challenges from other hostile editorialists. But he unequivocally declined Pryor's challenge and any others coming from his political adversaries.[51]

Although the incident appealed to southern audiences, it provided further fodder for northern critics of the *code duello*. By the mid-1850s, the *New York Herald* had already identified Pryor as a symbol of Southern Chivalry, and editor James Gordon Bennett frequently and unfavorably reported about the southern hothead.[52] Botts's offense, according to the *Herald*, was that he "had the courage and the manliness to oppose the wild fanaticism of Governor Wise and the Southern disunionists." While Pryor and the *Richmond Enquirer* engaged in political abuse "with a malignity without example," wrote Bennett, Botts had displayed "remarkable good sense and good taste" by avoiding the "ravings of his assailant." If he had indulged Pryor, it would have become a "settled doctrine" that anyone defending themselves against newspaper attacks would be open to challenges.[53]

The only Pryor duel that resulted in a violent conclusion occurred in early November 1856 in an encounter with Whig legislator Oswald B. Finney of Accomac County on the Eastern Shore. At Richmond's Exchange Hotel, which housed most legislators when the general assembly was in session, Pryor's friend Charles Irving became offended in an argument with Finney, and Pryor intervened by drawing a pistol and slapping Finney in the face.[54] Finney responded with a challenge, and the adversaries agreed to meet at a dueling ground a few miles outside Richmond, in Manchester, near the Free Bridge south of the James River.[55] Pryor wounded Finney on the first shot, with the bullet passing through his right hip. The injured man was taken to his lodgings at Ballard House in Richmond, where the bullet was removed. Although the wound was serious and painful, a reporter approvingly declared that both gentlemen had exhibited "much firmness and presence of mind."[56]

Richmond authorities, unable to prevent the duel, subsequently pursued prosecution. A week after the event, Pryor appeared before the city's mayor's court, which considered minor criminal cases. While Finney was still recovering from his injuries, Irving was also summoned as Pryor's second. The court sent the case to the hustings court, the next level in the local judicial system.[57] For a hearing the next day, the hustings courtroom was "thronged with spectators."[58] Once again, public opinion sympathized with the duelists. The seconds informed the mayor that the principals' disagreement was now resolved in an "entirely honorable and satisfactory" way for both men, with "amicable relations" now prevailing.[59] Nonetheless, on November 12 Pryor was indicted on misdemeanor charges.[60] Finney, however, insisted that Pryor should not be prosecuted and "be no further molested for any matter growing out of our late differences."[61] That settled matters, and the court issued a *nolle prosequi* order that ended the case on the condition that Pryor keep the peace and engage in no further duels during the next year.[62]

* * *

With a well-established reputation as a man of honor, in late 1859 Pryor became a candidate in the special election for Virginia's Fourth Congressional District, which included Petersburg and counties south of the city, in order to fill out the term of Rep. William O. Goode, who died in office in July. The campaign became the first occasion that the public heard Pryor's oratorical skills. One contemporary recalled him during this campaign as a "born orator" and a "thorough master of those rare persuasive powers that captivate and lead multitudes." With "erect and finely proportioned" features, the account continued, "his gestures [were] easy and graceful, his features mobile and expressive of every shade of emotion." The primary reason for Pryor's success as a speaker was the "charm of his oratory" and "his wonderfully organized vocal apparatus, which he played upon with the skill of a musical expert."[63] Another observer, writing fifty years after the campaign, remembered Pryor as having a "poetic imagination," the "basis of all true oratory." He had a "florid" though "superb" vocabulary and "kept company with the airy creatures of his exuberant imagination." Although his oratory "frequently soared above the comprehension of his audience, whose reading was limited," he found ways to reach them by combining a "logical mind with his poetic fancy" that saw "most deeply into human nature." Pryor possessed the "face, the figure, the dramatic air, the attitude, and the vocabulary" of a captivating speaker.[64]

Running for office for the first time, he adamantly defended the right of white southerners to expand slavery into new territories unconditionally. During the 1850s, the issue of whether slavery could be extended to new western territories became the flashpoint for sectional differences. In May 1854, the Kansas-Nebraska Act repealed the Missouri Compromise's guarantee that slavery would be excluded north of the 36°30′ line. The new law replaced these limitations on slavery extension with the principle of popular sovereignty, in which new territories would themselves decide whether to exclude slavery. In the Kansas Territory, popular sovereignty resulted in open warfare between proslavery and antislavery settlers. The Kansas-Nebraska Act outraged northerners, who saw it as an indication of the overweighted power of southern slaveholders. The new Republican Party, dedicated to limiting the expansion of slavery, now emerged and would eventually become the majority party in the North. Pryor allied himself with militant southern rights Democrats. By the late 1850s, southern radicals were insisting on the absolute sanctity of human property and the unlimited right of slaveholders to transport their enslaved to new territories. In a letter to the *Richmond Enquirer* in May 1859, Pryor declared that it was "primarily both the *right* and the *duty* of Congress to protect slavery in the Territories." Far from acting as a neutral mediator that would let voters decide the issue, the federal government, he believed, should defend slaveholders' property rights.[65]

Pryor's belligerence then moved from the field of honor and from the published word to the hustings. His exaggerated and bombastic style attracted voters. One North Carolinian traveled sixty miles on horseback to hear the silver-tongued orator speak. He described Pryor as a "wonderful" speaker, with a large vocabulary and a smooth rhetorical style. The Virginian's rhetorical flourishes mirrored his language, aggressive but attractive to his audience. Others agreed. "We have had no such speaking in Virginia since John Randolph's day," wrote one observer. Still another described Pryor as a "born orator" who exhibited "those rare persuasive powers that captivate and lead multitudes."[66] Virginians who heard him speak concluded that his success on the stump had much to do with his style. He had a "wonderfully organized vocal apparatus," said one observer, which he played with the "skill of a musical expert."[67]

Other, more critical observers found that Pryor was more style than substance. On September 21, 1859, after a district party convention nominated him for the Fourth District seat, another Democrat, Thomas F. Goode (no relation to William Goode), opposed him, claiming that Pryor was a creature of party operatives. According to this account, Pryor was "abounding in force and logic" and was able to keep the audience in "wrapt attention for an hour and a half." But Goode was better in content, in the "power and strength" of his words, and, unlike Pryor, dealt "less in tropes and figures." He used "stubborn facts" more often than Pryor, and, unlike his opponent, did not exhaust himself in "voice modulations and in turning nice periods."[68] Another observer agreed. After a debate at Prince Edward County Court House, he commented that Goode exhibited a "calm, dignified senatorial eloquence," while Pryor adopted a "lighter and more colloquial" style.[69] Nevertheless, Pryor won the special election in late October 1859. During the days immediately before the voting, abolitionist John Brown launched an assault on the federal arsenal at Harpers Ferry, Virginia, in an attempt to ignite a slave rebellion. Brown's raid set off alarm bells throughout the slaveholding South, all of which benefited Pryor's hardline radicalism.

In 1909, three years before her death, Sara Pryor released a second memoir, *My Day,* five years after her first memoir, *Reminiscences of War and Peace,* was published. She described how her family, following Roger Pryor's election to Congress in 1859, happily returned to Washington. Locating a large house on New York Avenue, they prepared themselves for a long stay. His constituents in Virginia were "devoted to him" and would "never supplant him with another." She asserted: "Of that, we might be sure. God granting life and health, we were going to be happy young people." Washington during the 1850s, she recalled, was like a "great village."[70] Sara frequently visited the Washington market, which was "abundantly supplied with the finest game and fish from the Eastern Shore of Maryland and Virginia, and the waters of the Potomac." There she found brant, ruddy duck, canvasback duck, sora, oysters, and terrapins.[71] But Sara noted that the city's advantages "caused us to ignore the real discomforts of life." These included cold winter days with "ice-laden street," the "whirlwinds of dust and driving rains of spring," the "swift-coming fierceness of summer heat," and the "rapid atmospheric changes which would give us all these extremes in one week, or even one day, until it became the part of prudence never to sally forth on any expedition without a fan, an overcoat, and an umbrella."[72]

In Washington, Pryor joined the young fire-eaters of the 1850s—proslavery, thoroughly modern in their sentiments, aggressive, outspoken, and quick to anger. He resembled such new, aggressive sectionalists as

South Carolinians Lawrence Keitt and William Porcher Miles, fellow Virginian Muscoe Garnett, and Mississippian and Arkansan Thomas C. Hindman.[73] Sometime during the 1850s, these men and others raised the stakes by making a case for disunion based on the compelling need to protect slavery.[74] By the mid-1850s, Pryor, still in his twenties, attracted newspaper attention as an up-and-coming southern-rights advocate.

Pryor's subsequent performance as an extremist in the Thirty-Sixth Congress, in late 1859 and early 1860, placed him at the center of North-South conflict. He was seated as a new representative in an atmosphere of intense conflict, what historian Joanne Freeman calls a "field of blood."[75] Republicans bore responsibility for John Brown's attack, Pryor declared in late December 1859 in one of his first congressional speeches. Republicans had lit a spark but then displayed "astonishment at the explosion," he asserted. After sowing the country with "publications of violence and sedition," they feigned surprise about the Harpers Ferry attack. Their strategy was to employ "tentative approaches and gradual exhaustion" rather than flushing out the "game too soon." Despite encouraging slave insurrection, the Virginian charged, Republicans were "quick to renounce their violent policy, and to affect the most pacific purposes." Understanding Republicans' true intentions, southern leaders realized "the artifice of ambition, working with the resources of hypocrisy," and were resolved to resist aggression.[76]

Pryor arrived in Washington during an acrimonious battle to elect the Speaker of the House. Republicans controlled a plurality of votes in the chamber but not enough to elect a Speaker without Democratic support. For eight weeks, between December 5, 1859, and February 1, 1860, congressmen remained deadlocked over the position. John Sherman of Ohio, the Republican candidate for Speaker, faced strong southern opposition because of his adamant opposition to the extension of slavery to new territories. In addition, along with sixty-seven other Republicans, he had signed a letter endorsing Hinton Rowan Helper's *The Impending Crisis,* which urged southern nonslaveholders to abandon support for slavery and join the Republican Party. This bitter debate ended only after they withdrew Sherman from consideration on February 1 and instead put forward moderate Republican William Pennington of New Jersey, who was elected Speaker.[77]

Nearly two months before the fracas with Lovejoy, Pryor had made himself a determined partisan in the fight over the election of a House Speaker. Tempers were frayed. On January 17, 1860, John Hickman, a Republican congressman from Pennsylvania, made the case for electing a Speaker by plurality rather than majority. Pryor responded heatedly. Hickman, he said, had spoken with a "disingenuousness which I confess amazed me, even from him." The Republicans' ultimate objective, he continued, was "not only to vanquish us, but to degrade us." The Pennsylvanian had added "the sting of personal insult to our defeat," and the Republicans' goal was to "dishonor the section" of slaveholding states. Hickman, exuding a "pharisaical superiority," had stigmatized "those who he represents to be disorganizers, agitators, disunionists." Hickman took offense that Pryor raised "a question of veracity."[78]

Earlier in January, the *New York Herald*'s James Gordon Bennett described Pryor as a "descent" from the great Virginia statesmen of the Revolutionary era. Although many had "hopes for Pryor; thought he might turn out well," they were sorely disappointed. He sought attention by speeches that were "as wordy, egotistical and sophomorical as were his dull editorials."[79] Weeks later the combative editor of the *New York Herald* again spotlighted Pryor, who had, Bennett said, forgotten "all the proprieties which obtain between gentlemen" by accusing Hickman of a "deliberate falsehood." He then mocked how a member of the Southern Chivalry acted with little honor. A "more ungentlemanly course of conduct," Bennett added, "could hardly be found" beyond New York City's notoriously rough neighborhood, the Five Points. Pryor attempted unsuccessfully to bully Hickman through the use of "vulgar and blackguard epithets." Virginians prided themselves on their gentlemanly behavior, but Pryor had crossed a line by transferring "his brutality and violence from the columns to the floor of Congress." He was a "mental shoulder-hitter, a philological pugilist, a moral bully." Bennett reminded readers that Pryor conducted frequent newspaper attacks that involved "the vilest personal abuse." The "stain which he affixed upon journalism now blots the records of Congress."[80]

The matter did not end there. On January 20, Pryor responded to Bennett on the House floor. The Virginian owed no responsibility of responding to "any utterance from that notorious individual." Pryor claimed that he had enough justification to "lash him until even his rhinoceros hide quivered with the pang of excoriated sensibility." Continuing this personal attack, he described Bennett as a "miscreant" and a "foul and filthy creature, whose name is the execration of both continents, and from whose contact truth and virtue shrink as from the touch of leprosy." Because of Bennett's "unutterable and unapproachable infamy," he declared, an attack from the *New York Herald* meant little to him.[81]

Pryor, as a first-term congressman, quickly established himself as a southern-rights hothead, and the encounter with Lovejoy should be viewed in this context. On April 11, 1860, Pryor delivered a challenge to John Potter on the floor of the House of Representatives. The challenge, as a representation of southern honor and northern restraint, sparked a national sensation. Pryor championed Chivalry and did combat with the supposed menace of Black Republicanism. Yet this also exposed Pryor and Chivalry to ridicule and an obvious clash of values on a national stage.

Once again, during the conflict with Potter, there was ample evidence that Pryor preferred bluster and newspaper exposure to physical violence. As the *New York Tribune* noted, the Virginian challenged Potter only because he was "well informed that Northern men do not fight duels" and that one likely would not occur. According to the newspaper, Pryor realized that the public spectacle of bullying had become an "exceedingly cheap method of avouching his own bravery."[82] Rumors abounded about a possible Pryor-Potter duel to the point that it was "difficult to command any attention" in Congress, "so general was the interest amid feeling on the subject." The Virginian's friends and fellow fire-eaters Miles and Keitt were absent from Congress, fueling rumors that a "hostile meeting" between Pryor and Potter would soon occur.

While Pryor laid low across the Potomac in Alexandria, Potter's whereabouts remained unknown.[83]

Subsequent negotiations were complicated. Because he was under police scrutiny and temporarily sheltered in Virginia, Pryor insisted that any duel occur outside of Washington. Two days later Potter's response contained a surprise. As the person challenged, he had the right to choose the weapons used and the duel's location. Potter insisted that it take place within the District of Columbia, the principals facing at a distance of four feet, and that the weapons would be "common" bowie knives of "equal weight and length of blade." A physically large man, Potter was better suited to hand-to-hand combat. He detested the "barbarous and inhuman mode of settling difficulties" and so refused to go along with the usual rules of the *code duello*. Indeed, the idea of using bowie knives struck at the very premises of the Southern Chivalry. Pryor's second, T. P. Chiseman, denounced the proposal not only as "vulgar, barbarous and inhuman" but also as inconsistent with the behavior of gentlemen and with "the notions of civilized society." In the meantime, Potter's second, civil engineer and explorer Frederick W. Lander, offered to fight Pryor himself and even gave him the choice of weapons. Ignoring Lander's offer, Pryor ended the negotiations with the lament that he was "unable to adjust the matter between our principals in the manner usual among gentlemen."[84]

Pryor's clash with Potter certainly added to his celebrity among white southerners. Dueling fed his appetite for celebrity, and southern newspapers avidly marketed him to their readers. Although the dispute ended as a farce, the episode appealed to southern audiences as an expression of manliness. Pryor represented "all that is dear to the Southern heart," said the *Richmond Enquirer*. "Wherever spoken," it added, "his name is the synonim [*sic*] of Southern Chivalry, generosity and devotion." As a congressman he "stood in the front rank of the intrepid defenders of the South," prepared "by word and deed, to repel the least encroachment upon her constitutional rights."[85]

In contrast, among northern audiences Pryor's attempt at a high-profile duel blew up in his face. The Republican press avidly mocked him. To the *New York Herald,* Pryor had been "cowed like a whipped cur."[86] Republicans enjoyed the rich result in which a northerner had humiliated Southern Chivalry. A northerner, Potter had refused to recognize the legitimacy of the *code duello.* Receiving a challenge from one the *Herald* called a "regular professor of the code," he had effectively ridiculed Pryor. In the end, observed the *Herald,* Pryor was forced to retreat "under the shelter of the code." In effect, the affair succeeded in exposing the Virginian as a "used up chevalier of the fighting school." For northern newspapers, the abortive duel represented something larger about the nature of southern radicals like Pryor. As one of them put it, southern demagogues had been "blustering and threatening for twenty years," and the only way to deal with them was "cold steel and cold lead."[87] The episode reinforced Republicans' view that southern radicals were bullies who were capable of delivering only empty threats. Pryor became a prime example of the "Southern hair triggered sensibility," but his extremism, and the fire-eaters' extremism, was leading to a national calamity. Northern newspapers also began to refer to the "coward Pryor."[88]

The episode thus exposed fundamental cultural differences about the meaning of honor and masculinity. The affair, concluded the *Tribune,* punctuated irreconcilable cultural differences between sections that evoked "mingled feelings of amazement, sorrow, and contempt."[89] Having deliberately inflamed the dispute with Potter, Pryor refused a duel because the weapons selected were "unusual." In reality, he was nothing more than a "braggart and a coward." He had entered the House in December 1859 with a reputation for a "rare skill in duello," an "extraordinary steadiness of nerve," and a "most unquestionable courage." With his anti-northern speeches, Pryor had lived up to his reputation for bluster and championed the "more turbulent and vituperative class of Southern members." Frequently, he "openly or covertly" used the threat of dueling in order to bully members and enhance his own reputation. Like the *Herald,* the *Tribune* maintained that the messy conclusion of the failed duel with Potter exposed secessionists as frauds. Northerners had no stomach for the "burlesque performances of the South in the dueling line." While Potter defended his right to free speech on the House floor, Pryor asserted a false code to attempt to squelch him. Lovejoy's speech, said the *Tribune,* was a "culminating point in the series of outrages heaped by the chivalry upon the Republicans from the commencement of the session." Pryor had "been seeking a fight with somebody all winter," but he now received his comeuppance. Assuming that Potter would refuse a challenge, he lacked any "stomach for a fair fight."[90]

Soon after the end of this episode, Potter returned to Congress to a standing ovation. Pryor, meanwhile, assumed his seat, according to the *Tribune,* with "an uneasy air, not a member noticing him on the way." Three or four fellow southern congressmen shook his hand, but only in the "most common-place way." In the lobby during breaks, fellow congressmen ignored the Virginian. The difference in how Potter and Pryor were treated offered "conclusive proof," said the *Tribune,* of the "general judgment" of their colleagues.[91]

For decades to come, the newspaper press often revisited the failed Potter-Pryor duel. During the war, in January 1864, one Connecticut newspaper referred to Pryor as "blustering," a man "whose cowardice was exposed by Mr. Potter."[92] Sixteen years after the affair, the *Alexandria Gazette* concluded that it had provided Pryor with his "first taste of national celebrity." At the same time, his celebration of a hair-triggered concern with personal honor and his tendency to exaggerate resulted in arrogant threats that he and southern radicals were unable to back up. Southern radicals were nothing more than demagogues, according to the *Chicago Tribune.* As the *New York Herald* put it, many northerners were fed up with them. That newspaper, having lost patience with southern bullying, resolved that southern honor was the "most transparent of Southern abstractions; and that Southern Chivalry, among Southern politicians, is Southern insolence and vulgarity."[93]

By the end of 1860, Pryor had become a relentless advocate of disunion. Nothing could avert this outcome, he believed. Like the "Last Generation" that historian Peter Carmichael describes, Pryor's youthful rebelliousness, fascination with modernity, and unrelenting sectional fervor drove a revolutionary ideology.[94] Republicans, with Lincoln's election, now controlled Congress and the presidency. They were consequently exhibiting their "spirit of sullen resolve to bring the issue to arbitrament of the sword." Virginians, Pryor advised, should "at once assume an attitude of armed expectation." Any "betrayal of infirm purpose," he wrote, "would only precipitate the collision." The South's "only safety" was a "union of the slaveholding States."[95] Nonetheless, the onset of war brought unanticipated consequences. During the 1860s and 1870s, Pryor experienced war, defeat, and reunion. In June 1876, the *Alexandria Gazette* described his resulting transition. If he would make "any more history," it commented, it would not be "as a fire-eater or a duelist; it will be rather as a scholar and a peace maker." Pryor earned the distinction of having been the "last southern fire eater to send a challenge to a northern mudsill."[96] Potter, who became known as "Bowie Knife Potter" and served three terms in the House, died in May 1899. He kept a bowie knife that Missouri Republicans had given him, inscribed, "Always ready for a Pryor engagement."[97]

2

THE CHEVALIER OF THE APPOMATTOX

Between June 1864 and April 1865, Yankee forces conducted a long siege of Petersburg, where they hoped to seal the Confederacy's fate by encircling Richmond and cutting off its railroad lifeline. Underground bartering of newspapers and sometimes tobacco between northern and southern soldiers on the front lines had become a "tacit convention," according to a contemporary.[1] Strict orders from both sides prohibited this trade, but these rules often went unobserved. On November 25, 1864, Roger Pryor approached the Union picket line at the trenches outside Petersburg, offering to trade newspapers. At the same moment, Brig. Gen. Byron M. Cutcheon, who served as division officer of the day, inspected the Union trenches. During his inspection, he noticed the approach of a Confederate officer, apparently a general, who was offering to trade copies of the *Richmond Whig* and *Richmond Examiner.* Although the officer identified himself only as "Capt. Brown," it was Pryor. He had resigned his officer's commission and reentered the Confederate army as a private more than a year earlier; nevertheless, he rode a horse and wore a general's insignia.

Chatting "without restraint," Pryor asked after old acquaintances and reminisced about Fort Sumter and "those early and momentous days of the war."[2] But he had walked into a trap; Yankee soldiers captured him and announced that the Virginian was their prisoner. On

November 27, two days after Pryor's seizure, two Union soldiers appeared at division headquarters with what was described as a "highly indignant" prisoner with long hair and "piercing" black eyes. The man insisted to the commanding northern officer, Brig. Gen. Robert B. Potter, that he was Brig. Gen. Roger A. Pryor and that he had been "basely trapped." Potter referred the matter to his superiors at the Army of the Potomac's headquarters at City Point, Virginia.[3]

The presidential election of 1860 witnessed a complete breakdown of the two-party system. Four candidates ran, each representing either North or South and none the entire nation. With the division of the Democrats into northern and southern wings, the antislavery Abraham Lincoln won an electoral plurality. Like other fire-eaters, Pryor enthusiastically supported Kentuckian John C. Breckinridge, the candidate of southern Democrats. In early September 1860, Pryor spoke to a crammed hall in Richmond, where the crowd greeted him with "deafening cheers." For three hours, according to the *Richmond Enquirer,* he commanded "the unbroken attention of the entire audience."[4] Later that month, in a speech in Norfolk, Pryor went even further by assailing Lincoln and promising his audience "to assas[s]inate, with his dagger, any President who shall attempt by force to prevent the secession of a Southern state." If anyone tried to coerce the seceding South, he promised to be the Brutus who would "plant a dagger in his heart."[5] Lincoln's election, representing a final straw for rabid secessionists, meant Republican control of the national government.

By late 1860, Pryor had become convinced that secession was inevitable. In a public letter published in late December, he declared that there was "no chance of preserving the Union" consistent with southern rights. The North would provide no guarantees, Pryor declared, and intended to pursue a "plan of coercion" that threatened southern rights. He sensed a "spirit of sullen resolve" on the part of Republicans to solve the conflict militarily. Pryor further urged Virginians immediately to adopt an "attitude of armed expectation."[6] In late December he introduced a resolution before Congress declaring that the "Union cannot be preserved by force, and that the attempts to use force would be destructive of Republican liberty." Although the resolution was soon tabled, Pryor had made his point.[7]

On February 4, 1861, the new Confederate States of America came into existence, establishing its capital in Montgomery, Alabama. After Lincoln's inauguration a month later, Pryor left Washington and returned to Virginia to promote the cause of secession. Meanwhile, most of the Upper South remained in the Union. In Virginia, voters elected a secession convention that met between February and April, but moderate unionists, who favored negotiation rather than disunion, held the upper hand. Pryor and other provocateurs attempted to sway the outcome by pushing a radical agenda.

Virginia remained deeply divided about secession. About a week after returning to the state, Pryor addressed a crowded meeting in Phoenix Hall, one of Petersburg's largest buildings. He announced that he favored the immediate secession of Virginia. Would Petersburg citizens submit to Black Republicans, he asked. "Never! Never!! Never!!" was the noisy response that "fairly shook the vast building."[8] Pryor's father, Theodorick, shared sentiments of southern rights with his son. In early 1861, he delivered a sermon in Petersburg that was, according to one account, "intensely political" in advocating disunion. About fifty of the congregants took offense and left the church in protest. As they exited, one of them cried out: "Traitor! Traitor to his country!" A "dreadful commotion" followed in which divisions in the congregation became apparent.[9]

Pryor became one of the better-known radicals who agitated while Virginia's convention was in session. In mid-March 1861, he addressed a large meeting in Richmond. Three hundred raucous supporters from Petersburg joined him aboard a special train to Richmond. The group carried the recently designed Confederate flag, a palmetto branch, and cockades, all symbols of secession. Pryor's speech in the capital occurred at the First African Church, previously a white Baptist sanctuary that, after whites abandoned it for another building, now housed Virginia's largest Black congregation. Because of its size, the African

Church served as the preferred location for the city's largest meetings. The building was filled to capacity, and "hearty cheers" greeted the speaker.[10] The old Union had ended, Pryor announced; seceding states would never return. He characterized the seventy-four-year-old lieutenant general Winfield Scott, a Virginian, Mexican War hero, and head of the US Army, as an "*apostate chief,*" while he called Lincoln "*a misshapen ape.*" Pryor declared himself prepared to lay down his life if Virginia would only imitate South Carolina's example.[11]

Pryor remained much in demand, and in late March he conducted a speaking tour across his congressional district, where he found his constituents "hungry" for secession.[12] Along with other disunionists, he focused his efforts on pressuring the convention. A speech in Brunswick County attracted a crowd that listened to Pryor for two hours of his "telling and convincing" rhetoric. When he finished, he was greeted by the "most enthusiastic and prolonged applause." The meeting concluded with resolutions demanding an ordinance of secession.[13]

The crisis deepened during the spring of 1861 with the military standoff between Confederate South Carolina and Union forces occupying Charleston harbor's Fort Sumter, one of several coastal forts operated by the US Army. When Lincoln tried to resupply the garrison with provisions and military supplies, Confederates demanded the fort's surrender. Secessionists from around the South traveled to the scene, both to witness and to participate in any outbreak of hostilities. Sensing the importance of the confrontation, Pryor rushed to Charleston, arriving on April 10, 1861.[14] Joining thousands of secessionists, he found a "large concourse" that included a brass band playing "Dixie." The crowd serenaded Pryor, urging him to speak. Needing little encouragement, he used his usual combination of personal appearance and rhetorical excess. According to diarist Mary Boykin Chesnut, Pryor "made great play with that long hair of his, which he is always tossing aside."[15] Delivering what Sara Pryor described as a "most impassioned and vehement speech," the congressman urged an immediate assault on Fort Sumter.[16] The case for secession lay less with the inadequacy of northern guarantees than with the "unutterable perfidy of the guarantors." He denounced any efforts at a compromise. If antislavery northerners could not fulfill the obligations of the Constitution, Pryor asked, how likely would they be to implement new constitutional guarantees that protected the South? An attack on the fort would propel Virginia into the Confederacy "in less than an hour by Shrewsbury clock," he declared. Virginia's secession was assured, he told Charlestonians, "*if you but strike a blow.*"[17]

While in Charleston, Pryor obtained an appointment to the volunteer staff of the Confederate commander, Gen. P. G. T. Beauregard. Pryor moved to the center of the conflict when Beauregard made him part of a four-member delegation that visited the fort on April 11 to demand its surrender. With him in this distinguished group were Texas senator Louis T. Wigfall, Charlestonian Stephen D. Lee, and South Carolina senator James Chesnut Jr.[18] Pryor prepared for the visit with his usual emphasis on performative appearance. The *New York Tribune* described him as representing the "very embodiment of Southern Chivalry." According to this account, he was "literally dressed to kill, bristling with bowie-knives and revolvers, like a walking arsenal." His bravado and bluster, however, proved dangerous. Once inside the fort, he saw what he thought was a glass of brandy. After he impulsively drank it, a US Army surgeon informed him that he had consumed a poisonous liquid. Pryor experienced what the surgeon called "purgings, pumping, and pukings" that indicated "how his bluster and impulsiveness might bring adverse consequences."[19]

Confederate president Jefferson Davis had ordered an assault on Fort Sumter only if its commander, Maj. Robert Anderson, refused to surrender. Pryor later claimed in an interview with historian William E. Dodd that Anderson had informed the delegation that a bombardment was unnecessary. Food had become so scarce that the garrison would be forced to surrender in two days. Pryor maintained that he suppressed this information for fear that Davis preferred a negotiated settlement. The four-man Confederate team instead informed Beauregard only that Anderson had refused surrender. As a result, an artillery attack followed from Fort Johnson in Charleston harbor. Though given the chance to fire the first shot, Pryor refused. The day after his delegation visited Fort Sumter, on April 12, Beauregard opened fire. After thirty-four hours' bombardment, Anderson surrendered.[20]

Lincoln responded to the Fort Sumter bombardment by calling for volunteers to invade South Carolina. His announcement converted most Upper South moderate unionists into reluctant secessionists. On April 17, the Virginia convention endorsed an ordinance of secession. Pryor learned the news as he was riding a train to join the Confederate Congress in Montgomery, Alabama.[21] Once there he spoke before a "dense mass of human beings" from the rotunda of the city's Exchange Hotel, according to a newspaper account. He praised God that he no longer participated in a political system under Black Republican control and their "wicked war" against the South.[22]

In Montgomery, Pryor praised Alabama secessionist William Lowndes Yancey's "talents and patriotism," calling him the "Patrick Henry of Southern Independence." Nonetheless, the two men disagreed about what the new Confederacy should look like. Three years earlier, in May 1858, at a southern commercial convention held in Montgomery, South Carolina journalist Leonidas W. Spratt introduced a proposal to reestablish the African slave trade. In a two-hour speech, Pryor opposed the proposal, which Yancey had endorsed. Despite his own "ardent and impulsive spirit," the Virginian thought Spratt's proposal went too far. Yancey responded bitterly to this, and the two men remained at odds.[23]

In May 1861, a statewide referendum overwhelmingly approved Virginia's secession. Secessionists controlled the legislature, militias, and most newspapers; the vote was a rubber stamp. Pryor also obtained a commission as a colonel with the 3rd Virginia Infantry. As a military commander, he emphasized style, personal appearance, and public display; his words, mannerisms, and public performance resonated with a southern public eager for secessionist heroes. Once again newspapers played a key role in Pryor's self-promotion. The *Richmond Daily Dispatch* told readers how a Georgia unit, after a drill, summoned him to speak. On horseback, he took off his cap and offered what the *Dispatch* called a few "brief, eloquent, and patriotic" words. Pryor also urged his soldiers to remain "patient and cool" and to trust their military leaders. Some Confederates, he warned, would not survive, but their death would be "honorable and glorious."[24]

Despite this heroic portrayal, Pryor, like other political appointees in both the Union and Rebel armies, had difficulty in managing and leading his regiment. Political influence and his reputation as a newspaperman and congressman had brought him his military rank.[25] He possessed no military training or experience. The 3rd Virginia comprised four existing militia companies. The oldest of them, the Portsmouth Riflemen, traced their origins to 1792 and claimed to be the oldest volunteer company in the state. Pryor's commission displaced the unit's commander since 1856, Col. James Hodge, who was transferred to the 14th Virginia. Some of the 3rd Virginia's men objected to the appointment of a politician as their commander.[26] Locals in the Norfolk area soon complained that Pryor's regiment was ill managed. In November 1861, a report appeared claiming that "nothing but anarchy" existed because the "whole populace" had to "bow to Roger A Pryor" and other "drunken officers" who led "half clothed" troops.[27]

Other soldiers grew unhappy about Pryor's leadership style. According to the 3rd Virginia's regimental historian, the colonel was overbearing and bullying and soon gained a reputation as "something of a martinet."[28] There remained militia men in the ranks who opposed disunion. During the secession referendum of May 1861, Norfolk County's Newton Marion Rifles, now a company in the 3rd Virginia, had voted overwhelmingly against disunion. Voting in Virginia remained *viva voce*, or by voice, and when the unit's opposition to secession became apparent, Pryor halted the voting. After delivering a "bitter and offensive speech," he briefly imprisoned unionists from the Rifles, though Governor Letcher soon ordered their release. A year later the Portsmouth National Grays, also in the 3rd Virginia, grew so unhappy with Pryor that eighty out of eighty-four men left the regiment once their enlistment terms expired.[29]

The reality was that Pryor was a capable fire-eater but no military commander. He was elected as a member of the new Confederacy's Provisional Congress in 1861 and reelected a year later. Since Pryor served on the important Committee on Military Affairs, the Confederacy's military leadership realized that someone like him needed special handling. His advantageous position ended in the spring of 1862, when the Confederate Congress prohibited its members from concurrently serving as military officers. Although he enjoyed widespread attention because of his bombast, Pryor knew little about how to earn his soldiers' respect.[30]

Despite these problems, Pryor was promoted to brigadier general on April 16, 1862. His promotion occurred during the bloody Peninsula Campaign, when Union major general George B. McClellan and the Army of the Potomac attempted to capture Richmond by invading Tidewater Virginia. Heavy losses among the ranks of Confederate brigadier generals meant that their successors were a mixed bag. By late 1862, sixteen of forty Rebel brigadier generals were recently promoted; thirteen of these, like Pryor, possessed no previous military experience. In the assessment of one historian, Pryor and a few others "lacked competence or the ability to head a brigade."[31] In fact, his promotion resulted more from an orchestrated lobbying campaign than from any battlefield accomplishment.[32]

Pryor's first combat experiences occurred early during the Peninsula Campaign. Pryor first saw action in the Battle of Williamsburg and then participated in the fierce fighting at the Battle of Fair Oaks (Seven Pines).[33] Newspaper accounts inflated his successes. His brigade, according to a correspondent for the *Richmond Dispatch,* had "won imperishable renown upon the bloody field." The writer described a "splendid scene" in which Pryor's soldiers "flung their battle flags to the breeze, advanced in quick time to the post assigned them." In a "warmly contested" battle, nowhere were the Yankees "more signally repulsed." This account especially praised Pryor, whose bearing and leadership stood out. He shared with his soldiers "their dangers and their perils," and he "stood calm and unmoved" while his men "seemed to gather something of his own spirit" by standing "firm and undaunted." Pryor had demonstrated his military leadership, affirmed the correspondent. He combined two "great requisites" of successful commanders—"good judgment, unmoved by the excitement of the hour; and firm, intrepid courage." Pryor handled his brigade with "consummate skill." In reality, the *Dispatch*'s account valorized the Virginian and exaggerated his successes. The hyperbolic language fed into the newspapers' continuing interest in the dashing young general.[34]

Among his soldiers, however, questions remained. A Louisiana officer complained that, after the Peninsula Campaign, his regiment was "more than half destroyed" because of what he called Pryor's "miserable and cowardly" leadership. Nothing more than a politician-general, the soldier wrote, Pryor deserved the "contempt of all soldiers." Because of his poor leadership, the brigade's organization became "confused," with resulting carnage. The soldier further maintained that during much of the fighting, Pryor remained "at a distance to the rear."[35] Ordinary soldiers, in any war, follow commanders who minimize battlefield casualties. To many of his troops, Pryor appeared more concerned about his reputation than about their well-being. According to this and other accounts, the general's incompetence had succeeded in self-promotion at his troops' expense.[36]

Subsequently, there was other evidence of Pryor's inability to manage the battlefield. In August 1862, Gen. Robert E. Lee sent the Army of Northern Virginia north, where it fought in the Battle of the Second Manassas. During the fighting, Pryor became separated from his brigade and encountered two Yankee soldiers. Posing as a northern soldier, he learned that he had strayed a mile and a half behind enemy lines. At some point the two northerners became suspicious and asked him to identify his regiment, brigade, and division. When Pryor hesitated, one of the Yankees leapt to his feet. "You are a damned rebel," he declared, "and my prisoner." Though now disadvantaged, Pryor gained the young soldiers' trust, and they lowered their guard. Once he learned that their rifles were unloaded, the Virginian plotted an escape strategy. An opportunity appeared when he spotted a rifle next to some dead and wounded men. Pryor grabbed the weapon and bayoneted the soldiers, killing one of them and wounding the other. Able to find his abandoned troops, he sent an aide to search the field hospitals to see if the bayoneted Yankee soldier had survived. According to a newspaper correspondent, Pryor was "anxious" to know more information, and when his aide located the wounded man, the general rode to the field hospital in order to visit him. Other contemporary accounts, however, claimed that he had killed both soldiers.[37]

There remains some inconsistency in Pryor's account. At least according to one eyewitness, during the encounter with the Yankee soldiers, the general appeared dressed in a private's uniform.[38] He later claimed that he had left his brigade seeking two or three regiments as reinforcements—an unlikely explanation. Even more suspicious was that Pryor was unarmed.[39] Five years later, in December 1867, he made a statement that appeared in the *Philadelphia Evening Telegraph*. In this version, Pryor recounted his temporary capture. After relinquishing his sword and giving his word that he would not attempt to escape, he was sent to the Union rear. Along the way and after "brisk conversation," he learned that the two young soldiers were unarmed, and it became a simple matter to grab a rifle with a fixed bayonet from a fallen soldier. In this account, he admitted that when he bayoneted one of his captors, the man "seemed to expire instantly." Pryor later told the army surgeon that he had "ran through the belly" of the other soldier. "He'll die, too," he informed the surgeon.[40]

Descriptions of the incident appeared in newspapers across the country. Northern accounts highlighted Pryor's battlefield deficiencies and called into question whether his performance abided by antebellum standards of honor. Southern newspapers, in contrast, magnified him into a hero.[41] After the war, when Pryor applied for a presidential pardon for his service in the Confederate Congress and army, a northern surgeon who had encountered him at Second Manassas, Pennsylvanian E. D. Donnelly, strongly objected. During the battle, Donnelly was tending to the wounded behind Confederate lines. Although he admitted that he left the hospital before he knew the fate of the second bayoneted soldier, he was convinced that the man eventually died; the two deaths, according to him, amounted to murder. Even worse, Pryor, according to Donnelly, had "boasted" of the killings.[42]

On the heels of his victory at Second Manassas, Lee continued north and across the Potomac about two weeks later, launching an invasion of Maryland. On September 17, 1862, during the bloodiest day in American history, his army fought McClellan's army in the Battle of Antietam. Pryor's brigade was composed of battle-hardened veterans from his 3rd Virginia, plus the 2nd, 5th, and 8th Florida Regiments. The brigade served under Maj. Gen. Richard H. "Fighting Dick" Anderson, whose division defended the center of the Confederate line at the Sunken Road. After Anderson suffered a wound in his thigh, Pryor, as the senior officer, was next in line to lead the division. At this point, according to historian Douglas Southall Freeman, Pryor's lack of military ability resulted in serious consequences. Antietam spotlighted his deficiencies. On both sides, Lincoln and Jefferson Davis found themselves obliged to permit the commissioning of political leaders as officers. Although in some cases the appointments brought positive results, in a majority of instances political officers were ill prepared to lead. As one of his biographers concludes, as a political general Pryor faced a "very sticky situation" at Antietam and was "in over his head." Another contemporary observer maintained that the general's "war activities . . . indicate bravery and determination, but [were] lacking . . . in skill and vigor-under-fire."[43] Subjected to Union flanking attacks, Pryor's brigade was mauled at the Sunken Road; some reports indicate that as many as three-quarters of his men became casualties.[44] Badly positioned and in disarray at the Sunken Road, Pryor's soldiers incurred heavy casualties from artillery and musket fire. The general's leadership, according to one historian of the battle, was "disjointed and without proper direction."[45] Another historian concludes that under Pryor's command, Anderson's division "dissolved as a military entity" and, according to a third scholar, "ceased to function as a unit." Maj. Gen. James Longstreet, commander of the corps that included Anderson's division, contended that Pryor did not realize that he had this new command responsibility, and as a result, the division did not fight in coordinated fashion. Nevertheless, Pryor had clearly failed as a commander.[46]

In the aftermath of the battle, thousands of suffering Confederates lay wounded. As was typical for Pryor, he intervened and, without approval from his commanders, rode to Union lines under a flag of truce. There he met with Maj. Gen. Thomas Francis Meagher, who led the Union Irish Brigade. Pryor brought along officers who were Irish, and they shared stories with Meagher. "It's a pity that we're fighting each other," the Union general said, "instead of whipping the world." A correspondent for the *New York Herald* noted that the two men, who were old acquaintances, had "quite an interesting conversation." He noted that Pryor appeared at the meeting dressed plainly in blue pants, gray shirt, and a "loose homespun coat" without anything to indicate his rank as a general. In contrast, Meagher wore an "appropriate uniform, of such texture and finish as his aristocratic tastes would naturally lead him to display." The Pryor-Meagher meeting in the end was for show only; neither side had approved these negotiations. Nonetheless, years later Pryor would describe the meeting as a "gallant" effort by two men from opposing armies who "grasped hands, in pledge of a friendship the shock of war could not break asunder, and in instinctive but unspoken presage of a community of country that returning peace should restore and perpetuate." Like many of Pryor's encounters, this meeting was performative.[47]

His failures at Antietam marked the end of Pryor's much-depleted brigade, and on November 10 Lee transferred what was left of it. Why he took Pryor's command away remains murky. Subsequently, some Yankee newspapers claimed that he was fired; other accounts asserted that he was charged with cowardice.[48] As was often the case with Lee, he worked in an opaque fashion that disguised his motives. His official explanation was that his decision resulted from the Confederate Congress's decision to reorganize troops so that more soldiers could serve under their own state's command.[49] Lee, writing to Pryor, told him that he "regretted" his loss of command and that he hoped that he would return to his Virginia troops so that "the country may derive the benefit of your zeal and activity."[50] Although this explanation served as the primary excuse for the loss of Pryor's command, an unspoken consideration undoubtedly was his battlefield performance. Historian Robert Krick describes Pryor as a "bewildered politician" who was far out of his depth and, to quote a cavalry colonel, "out of his element" on the battlefield.[51] As a member of the 3rd Virginia commented after Lee's purge, ordinary soldiers were now "clear" of "Old Pryor."[52] Later, other soldiers remembered that his inept leadership "was such that . . . Gen. Lee never suffered him to have another command during the War."[53]

Whatever the reason, Pryor became a general without a permanent command. In November 1862, Lee temporarily transferred him to the Department of North Carolina and Southern Virginia, which was commanded by Maj. Gen. Gustavus W. Smith and oversaw efforts to defend Richmond against the Yankee invaders. But Pryor had little intention of serving under Smith and instead maintained a pressure campaign seeking an independent command. In late 1862, the Army of Northern Virginia faced another Yankee invasion, this one under the command of Maj. Gen. Ambrose Burnside and leading to the bloody battle at Fredericksburg. Facing severe manpower needs in this area, Robert E. Lee told Pryor that troops were "more wanted here than there." Describing Pryor as "one of the best, most daring, and energetic officers in the army," Smith, in late November, dispatched him to the command of Maj. Gen. Samuel Gibbs French south of the James River. While exaggerating his military competence, Smith reminded French of Pryor's political influence. According to him, Pryor was "highly distinguished in civil life" and one of the "most influential men in the state, especially in his own section."

Under French, Pryor's main responsibility was to protect the Blackwater River region from Petersburg through northeastern North Carolina in order to assure the smooth flow of corn and bacon that sustained Confederate troops in Virginia. Sara subsequently inflated the importance of her husband's assignment. His troops, she maintained, kept Union forces "in check," and only by his "sleepless vigilance" were those forces kept at bay. The Yankees' "frequent sallies" from occupied

Suffolk were "always driven back with loss."[54] Roger again emphasized appearance and performance during this period. Years later a former Yankee infantryman remembered an encounter with the Virginian. The soldier, on picket duty near Suffolk, saw Pryor "dashing by" on a black horse. He was in his saddle, according to this recollection, "straight as an arrow," dressed in a dark gray uniform with a red sash around his waist. Pryor moved through the pine woods with the "rapidity of a Mazeppa and looked to me more like a Virginia fox hunter than a Confederate brigadier general."[55] Returned to his home region of Virginia, his main responsibilities were to curb Union depredations, secure supply routes, and forage for food and supplies.[56]

Nonetheless, Pryor remained unhappy with this temporary command, which he saw as a demotion. He resented having what his wife called an "inadequate force" but expected it would soon be augmented with reinforcements. Sara further remembered that her husband, exhibiting "symptoms of restlessness," was eager for a fight. In late January 1863, he told her that he had planned a "sally in the direction of the enemy." Yankees had become "entirely too impudent," the general said, though he proved unable to prevent further advances.[57]

In an action that occurred days earlier, Pryor once again exaggerated his successes. Although he claimed that he could pursue an "aggressive policy" if he had 3,000 more troops, his plea for a restored command was ignored.[58] Subsequent battlefield failures obscured whatever successes he claimed. By late January, Pryor's activities had drawn the attention of larger Yankee forces under Brig. Gen. Michael Corcoran and the Irish Legion, which tracked his movements and then attacked his forces about eight miles west of Suffolk in the Battle of Deserted House. Throughout the war, Sara often traveled close to the front in order to be with her husband. According to one account, the couple lodged at Webb's Crossing, a village in Southampton County, and even while the fighting raged within earshot, the general sat in a rocking chair away from his troops. Although Sara claimed that her husband "never left the saddle," according to this account, Pryor "never moved" from the rocker to return to his troops.[59]

Jefferson Davis.
Courtesy of the Virginia Museum of History & Culture, Richmond.

Newspapers once again portrayed him more favorably. Although the *Richmond Enquirer* described the Battle of Deserted House as "one of the most complete successes of the war," despite what the *Weekly National Intelligencer* called Pryor's "boasting," the evidence suggests otherwise. As a result of the battle, Union troops forced a withdrawal of Confederate forces farther into the Virginia interior. Some of Pryor's critics, contending that the engagement was a "useless battle, with unfortunate results," also claimed that he had fabricated his account. By the early spring of 1863, his temporary command was broken up, and the general returned to desk duty in Richmond.[60]

Thereafter, advertising his supposed military successes, Pryor unsuccessfully sought to return to the battlefield.[61] As Sara put it, her husband assumed that his "splendid service" guaranteed his return from exile. While the general gathered supporters and urged them to write President Davis to plead his case, he personally implored Davis, in a letter in April 1863, that he not be "denied participation" in the "struggles that are soon to determine the destinies of my country." He repeatedly contended that he was "embarrassed" by his demotion, though he claimed that it was not any "vanity of command" that motivated his desperate appeal. Rather, he maintained, he had a "single and sincere wish" to "contribute somewhat to the success of our cause."[62]

His father, Theodorick, met with Davis, urging him to reinstate his son to command. The Confederate president insisted that he opposed the disbanding of Pryor's brigade but that there was little he could do.[63] The general thus kept up his lobbying campaign. Sara recalled that, during the winter of 1863, her husband "never ceased" to remind Davis and Secretary of War James Seddon of his attempts to restore his brigade. Another contemporary described how Pryor had worked in congressional anterooms in Richmond for six months to obtain a command. But he was not an important enough politician, and Davis consequently brushed him off. In March 1863, tensions between the two men erupted after a story appeared in the *Richmond Examiner* that criticized the president for not using all available manpower in the war effort. Although Pryor long blamed Davis for his predicament,

Fitzhugh Lee.

Courtesy of the Virginia Museum of History & Culture, Richmond.

such opposition to reinstate him more likely came from Confederate military leaders hesitant to give him another command.[64]

Having missed crucial battles at Fredericksburg and Gettysburg, Pryor acted. Further meetings with the secretary of war led nowhere, only to further acrimony. When Pryor explained his "embarrassment" at lacking a command, Seddon suggested that while he had attempted to "manifest consideration and interest" in his military success, the reality was that the "generals under whom were Virginia brigades would not ask for and did not want him."[65] On August 8, 1863, Pryor relinquished his general's commission and joined the 3rd Virginia Cavalry as a scout in Maj. Gen. Fitzhugh Lee's division. Sara claimed that she implored him to become a civilian but that he insisted on serving, even as a private. "No," her husband explained, "I had something to do with bringing on this war. I must give myself to Virginia. She needs the help of all her sons. If there are too many brigadier-generals in the service,—it may be so,—certain it is there are not enough private soldiers."[66]

Years later, in notices that announced Pryor's death in March 1919, the narrative about his removal from the battlefield changed. A report in a Richmond newspaper, describing his war record as "brilliant," claimed that he had taken "a stand which is probably unprecedented in military history." Rather than Pryor having lost his command because of his military deficiencies, this account asserted that his views "conflicted with those of his superior officers." He then did the honorable thing by resigning his commission as a Confederate general. Like much of Pryor's record, this fundamentally misstated what actually had occurred.[67]

Pryor spent much of the winter of 1863–64 in rough and unpredictable circumstances. Sara recounts how her husband participated in a "dreadful tramp through the snow" in Confederate efforts to combat Union cavalry in southwestern Virginia. He "suffered cold and hunger, had slept on the ground without shelter," but had shared his blanket with his enslaved manservant, John. After months of duty with Fitz Lee, Pryor appeared in Petersburg during Christmas 1863 and surprised his wife; that he had no furlough seemed to make little difference. He also had $300 in gold that he gave to Sara for safekeeping; she quilted the money into her girdle.[68]

Throughout 1863–64, Pryor occupied a special status. "*Honorable, General, or Mr.:* How shall I address you?" Fitz Lee wrote. "Damn it, there's no difference!"[69] The 3rd Virginia Cavalry, according to a captured Yankee, consisted of five companies that included the "most respectable Virginians in the rebel service." Every member of the 3rd Regiment, a newspaper reported, claimed upper-class lineage. It included, according to this account, "the most conceited and egotistical braggarts that I ever encountered, and most of them are extremely ignorant."[70] Little is known about Pryor's activities during this period. By the fall of 1864, he had become attached to Robert E. Lee's headquarters; the *New York Times* described him as the general's "chief scout."[71] Still other observers claimed that he led a "corporal guard of scouts and bushwhackers."[72] Other sources variously described him as an "independent scout" or a "courier"; certainly, few people regarded Pryor as an ordinary private. Often, indeed, he was addressed as "General." Over time he worked independently, often behind Union lines. Sara recalled how, armed with a pass from Lee, Pryor's squad "set forth on his perilous scouting expedition, sometimes being absent a week at a time."[73] Other sources agree that Pryor had become a spy and was no longer, in effect, a private. A fellow Rebel called him "active, tireless, and daring in reconnaissances."[74]

On some occasions, his wife accompanied him, while on others he returned to his Petersburg family home. Sara remembered that Roger made it his base of activities and often returned on his gray horse, which he called Jubal Early. His mysterious activities kept him away for days. On one occasion, Sara recalled that he accidentally encountered a small Union party. He simply rode "gravely" by the troops, "as if he were an officer on inspection," and then galloped off out of distance of the "volley which followed the discovery of his ruse."[75]

In May 1864, Lt. Gen. Ulysses S. Grant, now commander of all Union armies, marched south toward Richmond in the bloody Overland Campaign. Confederate major general Bushrod Johnson, defending Richmond from Yankee forces to the east during May 1864, relied on Pryor for intelligence. By June 1864, Grant had pushed toward Richmond in a series of unrelenting and costly battles followed by flanking maneuvers. That summer the two sides settled into a long siege of Petersburg. Lee constantly probed Yankee entrenchments, and during these months, he used Pryor and a small squad to scout the enemy's positions. During these expeditions, Sara noted that Pryor had "adventures" and "narrow escapes." But he usually returned, sometimes after a week's absence, with useful intelligence.[76]

Union commanders took note of Pryor's activities. In August 1864, a Union officer, writing from eastern Virginia, described how Pryor's forces killed two Black cavalrymen who were repairing a telegraph line. In numerous other incidents, Confederate forces executed Black soldiers they captured, and this encounter, like those, was murder.[77] Union forces knew about Pryor, according to a description in his compiled service record. One Yankee account described him as General Lee's "chief scout" and a "dangerous man" who often worked behind northern lines. Pryor had inflicted "great harm" on Union forces by leading raids and plundering expeditions on their flanks and rear in search of arms, horses, and other supplies. This account noted that he had "made it his business to be at all times" near Yankee fortifications, often impersonating an officer to gain information. Among the activities in which Pryor reportedly took part were the informal contacts that occurred across the Petersburg siege lines, where he ostensibly sought to exchange newspapers but, the report claimed, was often gathering intelligence.[78]

On a cool autumn morning, Confederate major general Cadmus M. Wilcox, with pale face and quivering lips, paid a visit to Sara Pryor in Petersburg. He asked if her husband was home. He had not returned the night before, she responded, which she explained was not unusual because of his unorthodox schedule. "You have to know it," Wilcox said. "The General will not return. The Yankees caught him this morning."

When she looked out her window, Sara noticed Jubal Early standing in front her house; Roger was never separated from his horse. "Completely stunned" at this news, Sara described how her "heart sickened."[79]

Pryor's capture on November 27, 1864, caused a stir. Union commanders immediately recognized him, realizing that the capture of this fire-eating editor-politician was a public-relations coup. Yankee forces were in no hurry to release him. From City Point, Pryor boarded a steamer for Washington, held in a stateroom under armed guard. As was always true of how newspapers covered him, the reporter on hand provided a detailed physical description and stressed his appearance. He described how Pryor's hair "almost reached his shoulders, and upon his head he wore a stiff rim black hat." Pryor also wore a pair of cavalry boots that reached his knees. He kept the door to his private stateroom closed, "evidently being anxious to avoid the gaze of passengers."

When the ship arrived at Washington's Sixth Street Wharf, Pryor was "quietly seated" in his stateroom, smoking a cigar. Informed that it was time to leave, he responded in "theatrical style" and said, "Show the way; I am ready." A reporter following the story speculated that walking down Pennsylvania Avenue under guard might draw "unpleasant comparisons" with his "former swaggering" personality as a fire-eater.[80] Another eyewitness described him as "crestfallen and . . . disgusted with service."[81] Pryor was then transported by ship to Old Capitol Prison in Washington, attracting "much attention" when he was marched off to a cell. Even as a prisoner, he attracted newspaper coverage. The *New York Times* provided granular detail. Pryor was "but little hanged in his outward appearance," though his features were "darker from exposure." Nonetheless, the reporter believed that those who knew him "would have easily recognized him for his long flowing hair, sharp black eye, and bold and defiant look." When he arrived at the provost marshal's office in Washington, he "looked anxiously around," in search of "old friends in the crowd that were pushing forward to get a glimpse of him."[82]

From the capital, Pryor was transported to New York City; arriving in Brooklyn, he again attracted a crowd. According to one account, he was "jolly" while he ate breakfast with his captors. When he saw that his destination was Fort Lafayette, a facility that mostly housed Confederate political prisoners, he "became quite sober and reserved in his deportment," and a "violent shudder passed through his frame."[83] He was imprisoned there for nearly four months. During Pryor's incarceration, his wife could not visit, and only a few letters were exchanged. The Petersburg siege was discouraging, and Pryor, housed in a cell with twenty other prisoners with only a small grate for heating and cooking, became thoroughly demoralized. Sleeping on straw mats, the men took daily walks on the fort's ramparts. Pryor seemed to have little hope of release, and his imprisonment, he wrote his wife, deprived him of "every resource of happiness." In failing health, he later reported to his wife that his mind was "ill at ease from my solicitude for my family and my country."[84]

Pryor's release came only after the intervention of his network of Democratic newspaper editors. Washington McClean, Democratic partisan and Cincinnati journalist, led this lobbying campaign. McClean enlisted the aid of John W. Forney, another Democratic editor who had coedited the *Washington Union* with Pryor and who now served as clerk of the US Senate.[85] The two men wrote to Grant and Secretary of War Edwin M. Stanton, but both refused to release Pryor. Hearing about McClean's subsequent appeal directly to Lincoln, Stanton was emphatic. "He shall be hanged!" he declared, "Damn him!" Horace Greeley, Republican editor of the *New York Tribune* who had once called Pryor "the eloquent tribune of Virginia," wrote to the president and endorsed Pryor's release. Lincoln's old friend Joshua Speed joined in, assuring the president that McClean would "stake his fortune" on Pryor's willingness to honor a parole. Lincoln knew of Pryor's reputation as a firebrand editor and secessionist, even having occasionally used him as a foil during his speeches of the late 1850s.[86]

Forney and McClean visited the White House, where Lincoln heard them out. McClean made the case. Lincoln remembered accounts describing how Pryor, in a Richmond hospital, had been kind to wounded Union prisoners captured at Petersburg.[87] "The man who can do such kindness to an enemy," Forney recalled Lincoln saying, "cannot be

John W. Forney.
Library of Congress, Washington, DC.

cruel and revengeful." The president then scribbled some words on a card ordering Pryor's release and handed it to McClean. Despite his objections, Grant relented, telegramming Lincoln that the Virginian could "do us no harm now." After Pryor was released, an account described how he was "at large" in Washington, "looking almost unchanged since the old days when he blustered and bullied in Congress." The reporter also noted that Pryor, appearing on Pennsylvania Avenue, took "great pleasure in renewing old political and personal acquaintanceships." Forney even hosted Pryor in his Washington home, and the two visited the White House and received visits from other newspapermen.[88]

Nearly twenty-five years after Pryor's capture, in March 1889, the *New York World* published a controversial interview with the former Confederate. With what one newspaper called "striking frankness," Pryor maintained that the tariff issue, which had become the leading subject of the 1888 presidential election, could break up the "Solid South" by attracting southern voters to the Republican Party. Southern whites, he suggested, favored higher tariffs and protectionism now that the South had developed its mining and industrial resources and was competing globally. In addition, the region could profit from federal expenditures in the improvement of its transportation infrastructure. Once white southerners were reassured that Republicans would not interfere with their racial supremacy, he said, their solidly pro-Democratic voting habits would dissipate.[89]

Pryor's comments drew sharp criticism from southern newspapers. Though a lifelong Democrat, he had violated a political taboo in suggesting Republicans might be competitive in the South. He did not represent the region, said the *Charleston News and Courier,* and spoke with little more authority than other northerners.[90] Several weeks after Pryor's interview appeared, a small South Carolina newspaper, the *Abbeville Medium,* published an editorial declaring that he had no right to speak for white southerners. The editor, R. R. Hemphill, was a Confederate veteran who had belonged to Orr's Rifles, a South Carolina regiment posted on the Petersburg picket line in late November 1864, when

Pryor was imprisoned. Since by then he had lived outside the region for many years, Hemphill wrote, Pryor had lost touch with the South.

Hemphill further questioned Pryor's war record by publishing an eyewitness account about his capture in November 1864. According to Hemphill's version, Pryor appeared to go quietly, even affably once declared captured, locking arms with a Yankee soldier. He turned his back on "everything Southern," Hemphill declared, and left his comrades during the Confederate army's "darkest hour." Pryor was no more representative of southern sentiment than Benedict Arnold.[91]

As this version of Pryor's capture gained currency in newspapers across the nation, further details trickled out.[92] In early May 1889, Hemphill republished the account of another eyewitness, South Carolinian Oscar F. Chappell, who claimed that Pryor "deliberately deserted" to Union lines.[93] Stationed in a Confederate rifle pit with a good view of the incident, Chappell watched as Pryor rode up to his pit, stopping to take out a pair of binoculars to inspect the Yankee line. Desertion had become a common problem for Lee's forces by that time, Chappell recalled, and some deserters approached enemy lines by appearing to be exchanging newspapers and tobacco. So, when Pryor mentioned that he wanted to exchange newspapers, according to Chappell, he reminded the visitor that this violated the Confederate ban on interarmy bartering. "Oh, I am General Pryor; it's all right; hold my glasses a few minutes," he replied and then walked briskly toward the Yankee rifle pits. Using the binoculars, Chappell watched as a Yankee officer and two soldiers slowly came forward. Pryor and the northern officer shook hands and then they escorted him to Union lines amid cheers from the Yankee trenches.[94]

Responding in the *Charleston World* in late April 1889, Pryor described these charges as a "cruel and atrocious calumny." Newspaper exchanges were common on the front lines, he said, and served the purpose of intelligence gathering. Major General Burnside's corps had disappeared from the Petersburg front, and Pryor was attempting to determine the Yankee troops' location. He insisted that a Yankee officer had seized his right arm, and because his own pistol remained buttoned under his overcoat, he was prevented from resisting. Within range of fire from the Union line, Pryor said, "escape was simply impossible." He was "not ashamed to confess that my capture wrung from me tears of unutterable anguish."[95]

On May 11, 1889, Pryor's son, Roger Jr., published a pamphlet that included other eyewitness affidavits contradicting charges of desertion. General Wilcox, who commanded that portion of the Rebel line, confirmed that Pryor frequently exchanged newspapers. When he heard of the incident, Wilcox, after investigating, concluded that Pryor was deceived into capture.[96] The man who captured Pryor, Hollis Dudley of New Hampshire, was instructed to apprehend a Rebel soldier in retaliation for the capture and imprisonment about a month earlier of Massachusetts captain Henry S. Burrage when he attempted a newspaper exchange.[97] When Dudley heard that a Confederate officer wanted to exchange newspapers, he selected five marksmen from his regiment, ordering them to shoot the Rebel on his signal. Described as an athletic man, Dudley shoved a six-inch Smith and Wesson revolver against Pryor's chest and demanded his surrender.[98] Resistance would have been "sheer folly," Dudley recalled. Although Pryor was able to get his own revolver out from his coat, a Yankee soldier knocked it from his hand. Dudley kept the southerner's revolver, belt, and holster as souvenirs.[99] Most observers concluded that anyone charging Pryor with desertion, as the *New York Herald* put it, was wasting their breath. The war was over, it added, which meant that Americans should "lay aside personal prejudices and be just in judgement."[100]

In 1904, in her *Reminiscences of Peace and War,* Sara Pryor explained how the war had changed her husband. She recalled how, in May 1862, Roger and Mississippian L. Q. C. Lamar had fought together at the Battle of Williamsburg. Like Pryor, Lamar was a "warm secessionist." During the height of the bloody engagement, protected by a "stout oak" from incoming artillery fire, Lamar encountered her husband. "Oh, Pryor," he said, "what do you think now of the right of peaceable secession?"[101] Clearly, the experience of horrific warfare had undermined Pryor's obsession with honor and southern rights, and secessionist rhetoric seemed meaningless.

Although Pryor's version of his capture in November 1864 remained the dominant narrative, this episode illustrates the difficulty of a veteran remembering and explaining wartime trauma. Additionally, in some respects what occurred in the Petersburg trenches exemplified the failure of his war experience. Despite his celebrity as a newspaperman and politician who insisted on maintaining his personal honor, Pryor's participation in the war was at best erratic and at worst problematic. His militant masculinity, so common during the 1850s, could not be sustained on the battlefield.

Before, during, and immediately after the Civil War, Pryor's reputation as a protector of southern honor had vaulted him to national celebrity. He was, the *Philadelphia Evening Telegraph* sarcastically declared in September 1866, the "Chevalier of the Appomattox." He had ridden the hobby horse of honor toward a cataclysm that he did not fully comprehend. After secession, moreover, he had recruited young southerners to "do their duty to the 'sacred South.'" Yet his thunderous words encouraged them without endangering himself. "We had grown to believe that in some sequestered spot the gallant spirit of that brave man who didn't fight the duel with Potter of Wisconsin had breathed itself out, and gone into the presence of its Maker." In Pryor's perverted world, the "wicked" might "cease from troubling" and "shirk the contest." Although he "could there convince others that he was not a coward," his dream-like visions were "rudely dispelled." Still the *Evening Telegraph* predicted that, "now that the storm had passed," Pryor would "once more reappear upon the stage of public life."[102]

3

IN SEARCH OF RECONCILIATION

In January 1866, the newspaper editor and avid Republican Horace Greeley noted how quickly former Confederates had adjusted to peacetime. "Our gallant grey brothers," he sarcastically noted, were "routed, beaten, discomfited men, whose valor has almost atoned for the sins of the rebellion!" Even former Confederate generals had turned over a new leaf. P. G. T. Beauregard would "sell you a ticket from New Orleans to Jackson," while Simon Bolivar Buckner, commander of Rebel troops at Fort Donelson, was now a newspaper editor. Joining this august group was Roger A. Pryor, a "daily practitioner" in New York City courts and a prominent member of this "bold, vindictive and ambitious race of men."[1]

On October 5, 1867, in a letter to the *Richmond Whig,* Pryor began to offer a different picture of himself. After a Virginia newspaper labeled him a "Radical" who had turned his back on his native region, he responded. Renouncing political ambitions, he remained determined to pursue a legal career and to provide for his family. Pryor's approach—to urge fellow southerners to accept defeat—was not unique. Joseph E. Brown and James Longstreet, both former Confederate leaders, not only accepted defeat but also urged accommodation; a few ex-Rebels even joined the Republican Party. Like these men, Pryor urged accommodation; unlike them, he refused to advocate Reconstruction. But now he went beyond a repudiation of disunion. Instead, he wrote, he favored the rebuilding of the postwar South and reconciliation on the basis of "common interest and fraternal regard." He also believed that white southerners should accept the war's results, "adjust their ideas to the altered state of affairs," and recognize the civil and political rights of Black people. Pryor, in an explicit renunciation of his fire-eater rhetoric, urged southerners to express goodwill toward northerners, avoiding "the profitless agitations of political debate," and to focus on rebuilding their region.

Most controversial of Pryor's ideas appearing in his letter to the *Whig* was his advice that whites should accept freed people's new rights. He was no racial egalitarian; at best, he was a paternalist. African Americans, Pryor wrote, were not responsible "for the calamities we endure"; their attitudes toward whites mostly exhibited "kindness and subordination." He called for the preservation of a racial hierarchy in which what he called whites' intellectual superiority would help freed people achieve a "higher state of moral and intellectual development." Seeking race war in the aftermath of the Civil War was the "merest madness"; southern progress depended on racial peace. Pryor's point was less about racial paternalism than sectional reconciliation. Despite the war's bitter end, southern whites should seek "a complete and cordial reunion between the North and the South." Assuring the North that the white South would respect the sanctity of the Union was essential, as was the realization that northerners were "animated by far more just and liberal sentiments toward us than we are apt to suspect."

In this astonishing pivot, Pryor disavowed his fire-eating past. Admitting that secession and war had wreaked havoc on his home state, he now wanted to make amends for "the evil I contributed to bring upon the South" by becoming an intersectional intermediary who might advise "moderation and magnanimity." As Pryor well knew, fire-eater passion had led the South toward disaster; now, he wrote, "reason must conduct us back into the path of peace and prosperity." What the nation most needed was "repose" and a rejection of the "throes of political agitation." Alluding to his military experience, Pryor conceded his responsibility for war, though he never anticipated its "all-embracing ruin." War and disunion, he admitted, brought wasteful destruction, evident in "our wasted fields and desolated homes." In defeat, the former Confederate was "inwardly" dedicated "to the task of averting another such catastrophe, and to that end of cultivating a spirit of forbearance and good feeling among all classes and all sections of the country." The future, he asserted, lay in reconciliation.[2]

Remarkably, Pryor had remade himself. No longer living in Virginia, he had become a southern expatriate. The Roger Pryor of the 1850s was a hothead who opposed compromise and reconciliation and actively worked to destroy the Union. When he mentioned the "political agitation" before the Civil War, Pryor was referring to himself. But now that the world had changed, he had adapted to a postwar environment of uncertainty. Roger Pryor the fire-eater and Civil War general now became Roger Pryor the reconciliationist who urged mediation and peace over discord and war.

Paroled from Yankee imprisonment in March 1865, Pryor returned to his family in besieged Petersburg. Sara remembered her husband as "pale and thin," though also "devoutly thankful to be home." He brought with him two cans of pineapple, which he served to Confederate troops in the embattled cities on saucers and butter plates. He remained in Petersburg and strictly abided by his parole by avoiding any military participation. As Yankees tightened the vise around the city and finally broke through Confederate lines, Pryor and his family sheltered from the fighting. In early April 1865, they watched as Union troops marched through town singing "John Brown's Body." Once the city fell to occupation, like other residents, he depended on Yankee rations for survival. As *Frank Leslie's Illustrated* ironically put it, Pryor was "now the meekest of submissionists."[3] During the first months of Yankee occupation, northerners such as Elihu Washburne and Harry Wilson visited the former congressman.[4] On April 16, a day after Lincoln was assassinated, Pryor, with other leading Petersburg citizens, led a public meeting expressing grief and "abhorrence of the deed."[5]

Pryor remained a favorite subject for newspapers. Yet the disconnect between his personas, from secessionist to peacemaker, was too sudden for the northern press to accept immediately. The *New York Commercial Advertiser* characterized his release from Fort Lafayette as an "insult to every loyal citizen." As one of the people most responsible for "this accursed rebellion," declared an Ohio newspaper, Pryor should be tried for treason along with those who might "pay the penalty at the rope's end."[6] An Iowa newspaper, referring to two of Virginia's most insistent secessionists, proclaimed that the "day of the Henry A. Wises and Roger A. Pryors" had ended. The entire nation mourned fallen soldiers; the living included those scarred and mutilated by war. This horrible legacy provided a reminder of what fire-eaters, those "few swollen fools," had done.[7] Other northerners noted that Pryor had "come round at last to a more sensible way of thinking"; the war's "drubbing" had "done him good," and he now spoke "quite like a rational being."[8]

In the six months following the Confederate surrender, like many veterans, Pryor seemed broken and discouraged by his experiences of war and imprisonment. In May 1865, one contemporary described him as "terribly broken down" and appearing "to mourn the magnitude of his sin in helping to kindle and keep alive the recent rebellion."[9] During the occupation of Petersburg, Pryor encountered Union major general John A. Logan, with whom he had served in Congress. By happenstance, Logan's troops were quartered on Pryor's property. He and Logan conversed. With his long hair, clean-shaven face, and "bright but lustrous hazel eye[s]," Pryor more resembled a "college student than . . . a middle-aged, keen scholar." He had little sympathy with the recently captured Jefferson Davis. "I don't care much if they do catch him," Pryor said, "and yet I would not like to see him hung." He admitted to Logan that the South has been "fairly whipped," and Rebel troops still at large should give up the fight in defense of a "hopeless" struggle.[10]

Other accounts noted his transformation. Though only forty-six years old, Pryor was described by the *St. Louis Globe-Democrat* as a "conspicuous figure in public life" for two decades. In the abortive Potter duel, he enjoyed the distinction of having been "the last Southern fire-eater to send a challenge to a Northern mudsill." Like so many other observers, the newspaper noted the Virginian's still-striking appearance, which was "scarcely in keeping with his remarkable history." While Pryor's black hair was long, his face was "perfectly smooth," with a forehead that was "low and wide," eyes dark brown, and a manner that was "youthful, mild and captivating." If Pryor made any further history, it would not be as a hot-headed duelist. Rather, his main legacy would be as a "scholar and a peace-maker."[11]

Recent work by James J. Broomall, Peter Carmichael, Diane Miller Sommerville, and others have examined how veterans dealt with war trauma and injury.[12] Each dealt with the war's end differently, but few were unaffected. Sara Pryor later recalled that, during the months after the Confederate surrender, Roger suffered from malaria and an "ague" that had "fastened on him." She remembered that he "would sit for days in hopeless despair, looking out on the desolate landscape."[13] In May Pres. Andrew Johnson extended a blanket amnesty to all Confederates but required individual applications from Confederate leaders. In September 1865, Pryor went to Washington in search of presidential amnesty. One newspaper noted that the city's hotels were "crowded . . . with Southern patriots," noting that "among the most demonstrative" of the supplicants was Pryor.[14] Another paper declared sarcastically that Pryor, "known for his dueling propensities and for his treason," was in town seeking amnesty.[15] Nonetheless, the danger of federal prosecution remained, as there were, according to Sara, "men in power who constantly hinted at punishment and retribution."[16] Pryor's name appeared on the list of thirty-eight Confederate leaders that the US Circuit Court in Richmond kept on file for possible treason indictments. This cloud of suspicion remained over him until the collapse of the treason prosecutions in early 1869.[17]

In late 1865, a story appeared in several newspapers reporting that

Pryor was shopping a manuscript in New York. Although nothing further about the project subsequently appeared (and it was never published), these accounts provide some information about Pryor's transition from fire-eater. Entitled "*An Inside View of the Rebellion,*" the 500-page manuscript, according to one newspaper, depicted him as "far more philosophic and moderate in tone" than during the lead-up to the Civil War. The article described Pryor as rehabilitated, one who had "learned a good deal from the war" and, unlike the truculent fire-eater, had now adopted "milder personal manners." Further, the Virginian admitted in his manuscript that he acted "very unwisely and ridiculously" as a disunion agitator. His imprisonment during the end of the war proved crucial, according to this account. During his time at Fort Lafayette, Pryor came to realize the hopelessness of the Rebel cause. While there he befriended Confederate spy John Yates Beall, who later was tried by military commission and hanged on February 24, 1865. That experience and Beall's execution left Pryor, according to one source, "very deeply affected."[18] For him, a better future now lay outside of the South.[19]

Soon after the collapse of the Confederacy, Sara urged Roger to leave Virginia. She found an "obliging banker" to lend her $300 while she also pawned some of her jewelry to finance her husband's departure. Boarding a steamer, Roger headed to New York City.[20] He was in the city as early as July 1865. Upon his arrival, he used his connections with New York journalists and wrote anonymously for the *New York Daily News* at $25 per week; the job came through his old friend and prewar southern sympathizer Benjamin Wood. Pryor wrote enough for the *Daily News* to prompt one correspondent to describe him as the journal's "leading editor."[21] Another newspaper denounced Wood's Copperhead past and claimed that, after Pryor moved to New York, the "sallow-faced Virginian" had become "rather seedy."[22] Known around the city as the "Rebel Pryor," he nonetheless attempted to keep a low profile. Soon, however, he realized that he would be unable to provide for his family based on the "pitiful sum" that he earned at the *Daily News.* Pryor told his wife that he "renounced forever" what had been his "only object in life—fame, ambition, office." Meanwhile, he also suffered "ague and fever" with chills, fever, and nausea—"the worst I ever suffered." It was, he complained, "annoying to be so stricken just as one enters the fight."[23]

Intending to remain in New York only a week, Pryor lingered in the hopes of making a successful life. "Several gentlemen" suggested that he settle in the city permanently, and, encouraged by Wood, he studied for the bar. As it turned out, the exam was informal. While influential supporters among the attorneys in the city endorsed his application, the exam consisted of lunch with former congressman John B. Haskins. He enthusiastically endorsed Pryor's application in early December 1865.[24] An attorney without clients, Pryor found his new profession challenging. He also exploited his newspaper connections and ties to the Democratic Party to help garner work. Initially frustrated in locating office space, Pryor settled into a single room in lower Manhattan, which he rented for the nominal amount of one dollar a month. He soon discovered, remembered Sara, that his office had only unattractive furnishings, being a "perfectly bare" room with no carpet, "a plain uncovered table, and three chairs—one for myself, and the others for possible clients." This composed his "modest shingle soliciting the patronage of the public."[25]

Legal work was often discouraging. Pryor described the main obstacle to his success as a prevailing "prejudice against 'rebels.'" One lawyer refused to participate in a case with the ex-general because his hands were "yet red with loyal blood." Pryor hoped that he could survive and establish a legal care "if, meantime, I do not starve." In late December 1865, inhabiting a "lonely office" for Christmas, Pryor wrote that his prospects had improved with a case that earned him a $200 fee, but his hopes were "dashed to the ground" when the litigants settled out of court.[26] "I thought I had two *good* cases this week," he told Sara, "but my clients decided not to sue. . . . How weary I am of this."[27] After two and a half months of legal practice, he admitted to his wife that he had earned only $356, while he owed creditors in Washington and New York.[28] His legal practice was, he admitted, "uncertain" and had driven him to despair. "You can have no idea how miserable is my life here," he wrote. His work was "enough to make me crazy."[29]

Pryor's fortunes shifted after a visit sometime in early 1866 from Richard E. France, who operated a prosperous lottery business in Baltimore. France, referred by Wood, was Pryor's first real paying client.[30] After France confirmed that he wanted Pryor to represent him in bankruptcy proceedings, Pryor wondered how much his fee might be. To his surprise, France offered him a $1,000 retainer, with $500 if he took the case and another $500 if he won. Sara observed that because of this windfall, France had earned her "grateful blessing."[31] Still, Roger's business and income remained, as Sara learned, "very precarious," with a law practice that was growing "slowly but surely."[32] He complained, "I haven't a cent in the world," but his landlord seemed "to have faith in me, and is willing to wait until I earn something."[33] In October 1866, soon after he began practicing law, Pryor took on the case of the Rev. G. T. Williams, an Episcopal priest from Suffolk, Virginia, who was accused of pickpocketing while riding a tram in Manhattan. Thanks to Pryor, the case was dismissed, but the affair attracted some national newspaper coverage.[34] During his sojourn in New York City, Roger managed only one visit to his family in Petersburg. Not until July 1867 did Sara and the family join him and take up residence in Brooklyn. In March 1869, a newspaper noted that his law practice was "very good, and constantly increasing."[35] Within a few years, Pryor's work as a criminal defense attorney slowly grew; few cases were well paid.[36]

Only rarely did Pryor lose his composure during these years. In May 1871, he was involved in a case argued before the New York Superior Court, with Judge John H. McCunn presiding. After the trial concluded, according to one newspaper, he and the opposing counsel continued their courtroom argument. In a heated discussion, Pryor lost his temper. According to the article, he seized opposing counsel by the nose, "tweaked that organ violently," and grabbed him by his coat lapels. Pryor then gave the man a "vigorous shaking" while "showering epithets, remarkable for their vigor and terseness, upon his unfortunate head."[37]

Pryor's first trial attracting national attention involved the adultery case of Henry Ward Beecher, prominent public figure and pastor at the Plymouth Church in Brooklyn Heights. In August 1874, the noted newspaper editor and writer Theodore Tilton brought a lawsuit in Brooklyn City Court against Beecher, asking for damages of $100,000 (the equivalent of $2.5 million in 2022). Tilton charged that Beecher had participated in a "criminal intimacy" with the editor's wife, Elizabeth Richards Tilton. A subsequent church investigation absolved Beecher of any wrongdoing. In late 1874, Pryor joined Tilton's legal team, joining four other attorneys that included William Fullerton, considered one of New York's leading criminal defense lawyers.

The six-month-long case, which became one of the nineteenth century's famous trials, attracted a national audience and earned regular newspaper coverage. Tickets to the trial were sold on the black market; thousands of spectators were turned away.[38] Although most observers concluded that Beecher was an adulterer, the trial resulted in a hung jury in July 1875. The Plymouth Church subsequently blamed Tilton, a member of the congregation. Pryor appeared at the church in early November and read a statement defending his client's conduct. Although a "most impressive silence" greeted the statement, Tilton was expelled from the church.[39] Sara Pryor maintained that the case enabled Roger to transition from "rebel politician and soldier" to lawyer. It also further expanded her husband's following among journalists.[40]

Pryor's charisma and ability to use his physical appearance became part of his courtroom advocacy. A Milwaukee reporter described him as having a "strange, grotesque, yet attractive face, whose courtesy is never at fault."[41] Another found himself "at a loss" for where to begin his characterization. His talent for persuading juries was obvious "from the very first, though formal, sentence that exploded from General Pryor's lips." He relied on "surcharged batteries of personal electricity" and a "volcanic torrent of speech"—though the "most dexterous reporters could hardly follow him." His courtroom energy erupted "from every pore of his body, as well as out of his mouth, eyes, and finger ends." His diction, delivered with "headlong speed," was "perfect in precision and force, and no less in elegance."[42] The *New York Tribune* called Pryor "an eloquent orator" with an "eccentric" delivery, "earnest and profuse" gesticulations, and "nervously excitable" manner. Pryor also modulated the volume of his delivery for effect. First bending forward and lowering his voice to a whisper, he then used his "Indian-like figure" to straighten up while his face lit up with "intense earnestness" and his voice rang out "clearly as a bell." Pryor spoke slowly, adding long pauses between his sentences, but at other points "the words flow[ed] from his mouth without effort." His delivery, said the reporter, was "wonderfully rapid." Pryor nervously played "lightly" with his eyeglasses and swung them around his finger, ending by placing them "upon his nose and peering curiously over them." In a subsequent gesture, he wiped his glasses with a handkerchief, which he flung "with a quick motion across the table."[43]

A decade after the Beecher-Tilton case, in 1883, a Wisconsin reporter expressed more skepticism about Pryor's performance. The journalist admitted that the attorney's face was "so striking" that those unacquainted with him were "hardly indifferent to its mobile irregularity." What others saw as Pryor's energy was really an "uneasiness" that was "constantly revealed in his countenance," especially the "somewhat distortive thrusting of the under lip." Of greater significance than Pryor's appearance was this reporter's account of his role in the proceedings, which he joined only after he was "allowed to attach himself to the case." Money was not a motive; the lawyers on Tilton's team made a "comparatively small sum" from the case. For Pryor, it was mainly about exposure. Less than a decade after he moved to New York City, he "had not yet gained any foothold here and was naturally anxious to get before the public." Pryor had little role in the trial, and his "brilliant oratory" was lost to his "excited nerves." The main value of his participation was a "connection with a celebrated case" that would garner him more business.[44]

The Tilton-Beecher trial became the first of a series of celebrity cases involving Pryor that together indicated the disappearance of personal honor as a guiding principle. Some of his clients, like Tilton, were involved in marital and divorce issues.[45] Still others were political and, in particular, expressed a rising sympathy for workers and unions. In May 1886, during a strike against McCormick Harvesting Machine Company, a bomb exploded at a labor rally in Haymarket Square in Chicago, followed by a gun battle between police and strikers. Seven policeman and at least four strikers, probably more, lay dead afterward. Chicago authorities prosecuted the accused perpetrators; in August 1886 eight defendants were tried and sentenced to death. Pryor became involved on its appeal to the US Supreme Court, which heard arguments in September 1887. Although the court denied the appeal in November, Pryor had gained a reputation as a union defender.[46]

Although Pryor had sworn off further officeholding, he was disqualified by Section III of the Fourteenth Amendment, which barred former Confederate leaders from federal officeholding. In order to restore this right to an individual, a two-thirds vote in both the House of Representatives and the Senate was required; Pryor regained his qualification in March 1880.[47] Nonetheless, during the 1870s, he became involved in city politics, often mixing in business. Had he remained in Virginia, like a few former Confederates, he might have become a Republican. But he had remained a Democrat, perhaps because of his connections with Democratic editors. In New York City, Tammany Hall, the dominant political organization there, controlled the local party. In ideology, Pryor still believed in limited government. During the postwar era, like other Tammany Democrats, he expanded associations with Irish immigrants and, to some extent, with organized labor. As one historian writes, Pryor became a "sachem of Tammany Hall." He served as a New York delegate to the 1876 Democratic National Convention and on the 1886 convention's general committee. He subsequently remained a loyal Democratic partisan. During the 1880s, when activists urged civil-service reform—involving an end to extensive party patronage—he followed Tammany's lead and opposed it. Pryor stood by the "memorable formula," he told one group, that "'to the victors belong the spoils.'"[48] He supported Democratic presidential candidates, even the 1880 nominee, Winfield Scott Hancock, whom he had fought against at Antietam.[49]

Pryor's alliance with Tammany brought a close association with the Irish diaspora in New York City. John Mitchel, a prominent Irish nationalist, had arrived in the United States during the 1850s and became an ardent proslavery advocate. Subsequently, he favored the Confederate cause as an Irish Copperhead; two of his sons died fighting for the Rebel cause. In addition, Mitchel was closely associated with Benjamin Wood and helped edit the *Daily News*. An Anglophobe, Pryor naturally embraced the Irish nationalist cause.[50] The *New York Sun* described his "great influence" among workers and unions; his opinion was "respected as is that of no other man." Among Irish residents, in addition, Pryor was influential because of his anti-Know-Nothing stance during the mid-1850s. According to this account, they had become "among his best friends, and many of the most prominent of them are his best clients."[51]

In 1883, Pryor helped defend Patrick O'Donnell, immigrant to the United States and a naturalized US citizen—but also a member of the violent Irish nationalist organization the Invincibles. In May 1882, this secret group had murdered Lord Frederick Cavendish, chief secretary for Ireland, and Thomas Henry Burke, the permanent undersecretary, in Dublin. After Invincibles leader James Carey testified for the prosecution, five nationalists were convicted and hanged in May and June 1883. Subsequently, an English court convicted O'Donnell of killing Carey during the notorious Phoenix Park murders and sentenced him to death. Although Pryor traveled to London, his attempt to intervene in the case failed, and O'Donnell was hanged on December 17, 1883. Another Invincible, Patrick Tynan, fled to New York, where Pryor successfully prevented his extradition. Both the O'Donnell and Tynan cases greatly elevated Pryor's standing among Irish nationalist organizations, while the cases brought him fees of $1,500 (equivalent to $42,000 in 2022).[52]

During the 1880s, Pryor worked closely with former Union major general Benjamin Butler. They became allied in early 1876 during the impeachment of Adelbert Ames, Republican governor of Mississippi, who was Butler's son-in-law. Democrats had swept that state's elections in 1876 and, armed with an impregnable majority, pursued Ames with trumped-up charges.[53] Butler wrote a letter of introduction for Pryor to Ames, saying "you will like him immensely," adding that "if any man can save you he will." But when Pryor arrived in Jackson, Mississippi's capital, he discovered that he faced a hopeless situation. He quickly negotiated Ames's resignation in order to avoid an impeachment and trial.[54]

In 1881, Pryor and Butler formed a law partnership. Their paths had already crossed during the war, but in later years the two men knew each other because they were both criminal defense attorneys. Their partnership also extended into politics, though Butler, unlike Pryor, was a Republican. In 1880, Pryor persuaded him to cross party lines in order to support Hancock, his former comrade in arms, during his campaign for president as a Democrat. Two years later, when Butler ran for governor of Massachusetts, he switched party affiliation and became a Democrat. Pryor supported him after Butler appealed for his help as a "thoroughly reconstructed union loving rebel." He greeted his partner's election enthusiastically. "As a Democrat," Pryor told partisans in November 1882, he favored the "overthrow of pseudo Republicanism in its stronghold." On the other hand, "as a man I exalt over the well-earned trump of my friend."[55] Subsequently, with Pryor's support, Butler ran an unsuccessful campaign for the presidency.[56] The two men shared another attribute: both adopted the cause of Irish immigrants and workers. In 1884, the *New York Sun* described Pryor's "great influence" in New York with the "workingmen element" and noted that, with the Irish, he was "equally influential." Both groups were key to New York Democratic politics, and his standing as an attorney was reflected in his political influence.[57]

In contrast to his uncompromising extremism during the 1850s, Pryor became a skilled negotiator in his postwar career. A telling example of this transformation occurred in August 1874, when he heard from Paul Octave Hébert, a former governor of Louisiana and Confederate general who became a Republican after the war. In 1874, U. S. Grant appointed Hébert to a position on the US Board of Engineers for the Mississippi River Commission, which was responsible for maintaining the river's levees. In July, the *New York World* denounced the appointment, calling Hébert "bankrupt in fortune and character." Considering challenging *World* editor Manton Marble to a duel, Hébert consulted with Pryor in New York. Once an accomplished defender of personal honor, Pryor now offered different advice. The episode, had it occurred decades earlier, would have prompted a challenge. But did Hébert realize the consequences of participating in a duel in New York? Within hours of issuing a challenge, Pryor warned, the Louisianan would be in a New York jail, "a very uncomfortable place for a gentleman of your tastes and habits." Then, unless he paid $50,000 bail, he would probably remain in jail for several days. Hearing Pryor's analysis, Hébert's face "grew visibly longer and his moustache stiffer at this appalling picture," according to a newspaper account. The aggrieved Hébert asked if there was any way he could obtain satisfaction. Pryor suggested a libel suit, promising a settlement of between five cents and $5,000. In August 1874, Hébert filed a libel suit against Marble in New York's federal court for $50,000. The case went nowhere, but Hébert found a face-saving way to end the matter.[58] Pryor saw no point in insisting on personal honor but rather embraced the legal process as the proper way to preserve the favor of public opinion. More broadly, it was increasingly the case that white southerners resolved conflict and maintained their manhood and honor through the law.

While establishing himself as a leading New York lawyer, Pryor avidly participated in the city's social scene, joining the Manhattan Club and appearing frequently in local newspapers' social pages. He qualified for this high social standing because his law practice brought him fortune as well as fame. In 1886, he was reported as earning an annual salary of $20,000 (equivalent to $598,000 in 2022), while he earned a substantial return on his investment in railroad bonds. In the mid-1880s, he moved his family from the house in Brooklyn Heights to a more spacious residence at 68 East Thirty-Third Street in Manhattan.[59]

In April 1891, a reporter for the *North American* toured the homes of expatriate southerners—among them, the New York City residence of Roger and Sara Pryor. He noted the "remarkable strength of the southern colony," which he estimated numbered in the thousands. The Pryors, one of the most successful of these exiles, lived in a large brownstone, "furnished throughout in exquisite taste." Prominent in Manhattan society, Sara was described as a "calm, dignified lady, whose gentleness is manifest in every movement." On Sundays, the Pryors often hosted an open house that attracted the city's elite. Describing their home in detail, the reporter noted several parlors, which were "very stately, handsome apartments," with "every piece of furniture and bric-a-brac" reflecting the couple's "perfect taste." The main parlor had a colonial mantel, with two massive, antique candlesticks. The color scheme in this room was "soft terra cotta, lighted with a shade of pale pink," while the walls, ceilings, and the room's heavy carpet were in the same color. Fastened to the wall in a corner was a cabinet filled with Sara's Worcester and Dresden china. While easy chairs filled up the room's other corners, there were mementoes everywhere. Roger's large home office occupied the front section of the second floor.[60]

Moving in exalted circles among upper-class Manhattanites, Roger was usually called "General Pryor."[61] Many of the New York elite, including former Union general George B. McClellan, attended when the Pryors introduced their two daughters to society; that evening they offered tea from a silver service with the inscription, "Presented by the State of Virginia to Colonel Roger A. Pryor for Valorous Service in the Confederate Army."[62] According to one account, McClellan quipped that he could "certify to the valor mentioned," since much of Pryor's combat experience occurred against McClellan's troops.[63] A popular after-dinner speaker, Pryor socialized with a broad spectrum of the New York political establishment and conversed easily with current and former generals like William T. Sherman and U. S. Grant.[64] In October 1890 journalist John Russell Young hosted a dinner in Pryor's honor at New York's Astor House. The guest list included luminaries such as then–former president Grover Cleveland, utopian novelist Henry George, Mark Twain, and cartoonist Thomas Nast. Also present was Sherman. At one point in the dinner, the general laid his hand on Sara

Pryor's shoulder. "We would have done all this for him long ago," he remarked, "but he had to be such a rebel!"[65]

Eight years after Grant's death in 1885, Pryor participated in an observance of the former president's birthday. Sitting at the head table in a banquet at the Waldorf Hotel, he was warmly welcomed. Former brigadier general Horace Porter described him as a "distinguished general . . . who fought with us in the war—but not on the same side." Porter found it "astounding" how much "you like a man after you fight him!" Pryor, assuming the lectern, assessed Grant's "unchequered career of conquest." Despite having been "confronted by a foe of unsurpassed courage and constancy," the Union commander overcame all obstacles in such a fashion to associate him with the great military leaders of world history. It was Grant's "strong arm" that upheld the Union "in the instant of imminent overthrow." Most important, according to this former Confederate, was that Grant preserved the Union and "rendered to the cause of liberty and civilization as transcendent a service as any recorded in the annals of human achievement."[66]

In December 1886, Atlanta journalist Henry W. Grady announced to an audience of white northerners at the New England Society of New York that a "New South" was rooted in post–Civil War reconciliation. He had spent the latter part of the 1870s in New York City and was abreast of the southern white community there. For about a decade before Grady's famous speech, which a New York newspaper described as the "best speech that has been delivered in many years," Pryor had advocated sectional reconciliation.[67] Like Grady and unlike many Gilded Age reconciliationists, he addressed a primarily northern audience and declared, by his own example, a fundamental change in how southern men considered nationality, war, and sectional integration.

Pryor advanced this new message as early as December 1873, when he was the lead speaker at a meeting of the Long Island Historical Society. Using as his topic "The Negro Question," he outlined emancipation's ramifications on the South. In addressing this topic before a northern audience, Pryor began a decades-long attempt to interpret the post–Civil War South to outsiders. He brought a mixed message. On the one hand, he sprinkled common racial stereotypes throughout his speech. Freed people, Pryor said, were ignorant, "idle and improvident, and totally unfit for [the] changes" that came with freedom. Thrust into the national spotlight, he continued, they were "looked upon with little favor" either by northern or southern whites. Nevertheless, the South's and the nation's future lay in racial peace. Former slaves were "human beings, parcel of the population and political community of the nation," but they presented a common, national challenge and created a "subject of anxious deliberation to every humane and intelligent man." The welfare of southern whites, Pryor explained, was "intimately connected" with Black welfare, and either through impulses of "generous enthusiasm" or "sordid self-interest," Americans needed to encourage racial progress. If the freed people became "thrifty and industrious," they would contribute to national prosperity. If they became "enlightened" in their "understanding" and "pure" in their morality, "in precisely the same ratio" would they help sharpen a broader enlightenment. But if they were "idle and impure or blind" in intellect, African Americans would "despoil our wealth," while their ignorance would drag down the nation as their "depravity soil[ed] and debase[d] our virtue." Although unquestionably racist, this was, for the late nineteenth century, an unusually progressive position for a white southerner to take in the war's immediate aftermath. Like his views about other aspects of sectional conflict and stability, here he advanced a flexible and pragmatic consideration of race in the postwar South.

Unlike many others, Pryor saw hope in the postemancipation era. The Black man's virtues, he asserted, "were his own," while "his vices were his heritage, and the former outnumbered the latter." In their experience, Black people possessed no inherent deficiencies and were capable of attaining civilization's "highest achievements." Repeating a common trope among southern whites, Pryor praised former slaves' faithfulness to their masters during the Civil War; often they were the "guardian angels" of white households. To their credit, according to

Pryor, freed people were also deeply religious. Perhaps his most surprising assertion was that the major obstacle to racial progress lay in a "prejudice of race and color" that existed across the nation. Equalizing this problem across the sectional divide, Pryor reminded white northerners about how white Americans shared a common racist bond. African Americans felt the sting of racism in public spaces; in hotels, theaters, and churches; and even in the graveyard, where the "bones of no negro rests in your beautiful cemetery." Despite the white South's opposition to Black political participation, their record as leaders was no worse than that of white politicians. No African Americans were connected to the corruption of the Grant administration, Pryor pointed out, and the performance of the Reconstruction South Carolina legislature compared favorably with northern legislatures.[68]

Pryor had to tread artfully in delivering this address, which attracted wide national attention. In effect, he had crafted a version of sectional reconciliation that, as an expatriate, would explain the South to the North in terms that northerners understood. There was no one model for reconciliation; even the very term remained contested. Responses to Pryor's address varied by region. Many southern newspapers objected to his attempt to represent the views of southern whites. They questioned his loyalty to the southern insistence on racial orthodoxy; yet Pryor, as an expatriate in the North, felt free to express unconventional views. He had performed "a complete somersault on the negro question," claimed the *Vicksburg Herald*. Previously, Pryor "did not prove much of a prophet," and fifty years hence Americans would see the "fallacy of his predictions now." *Vide et crede*—see and believe—provided the *Herald*'s concluding assessment.[69] More vitriolic responses came from border states. The *Weekly Caucasian*, published in Lexington, Missouri, described Pryor as a "Jackanape," a nineteenth-century insult for an impudent or conceited person. He was a "long-haired, lank-jawed, cadaverous-hued blatherskite" who served the Confederacy but "was never heard of as a soldier." Using a racial slur, the newspaper declared that Pryor had "just bloomed out the savoriest-scent niggerite of them all."[70] The *Cincinnati Enquirer*, though less openly racist, condemned his message as well. Calling the address a "remarkable lecture upon the negro race," the newspaper questioned Pryor's credibility. He had, after all, belonged to the "ultra Southern Rights school of politics" and was a "staunch champion of the institution of slavery." It seemed "rather odd to hear him now utter such sentiments as these." In effect, the newspaper claimed, Pryor had become an abolitionist, though no northerner had ever taken this "extreme position in regard to negro capacity." In particular, the *Enquirer* asserted, Black people were unable to understand the "qualities of high civilization" and were "contented with their inferior position until freedom was forced upon them from without."[71]

Some northern critics, however, claimed that Pryor's ideas indicated changed attitudes among southern whites. Now and then a southerner learned "wisdom by experience," commented an Illinois newspaper. Pryor had been a "radical member of the oligarchy, whose aim it was to perpetuate slavery." Now, "thoroughly cured of his folly," he presented a new attitude. By providing a "just tribute to the despised negro," Pryor accepted the "situation in a frank and manly way."[72] A Wisconsin newspaper took the same approach. Pryor's ideas about Black people offered a "remarkable instance of the changes that time works, that an ultra southerner should become the defender and advocate of a negro before a northern audience." It added, "Probably no friend of the colored race ever spoke more strongly in their behalf than did General Roger A. Pryor."[73]

Eleven years later, in June 1884, a group of the New York Colored Democratic Association invited Pryor to speak. Not surprisingly, he declined the invitation by claiming that some "inconsistent engagement" made his appearance impossible. But he made a statement available to the press expressing his views. Democrats, he maintained, were "accidentally deflected" from the party's commitment to the "equality of human right and universality of human liberty." Now, with emancipation and the end of slavery, this "unnatural and ill-omened alliance" between Democrats and slavery had ended, and he greeted "the colored man to political fellowship as an equal and worthy member of the party."[74]

In October 1875, at a veterans' gathering in Elizabeth, New Jersey, Pryor offered his version of what sectional reconciliation might mean. The South fought the Civil War in defense of states' rights and the right of secession, he said. Northerners believed that they could limit the expansion of slavery; white southerners thought it was a "domestic institution to be managed by ourselves." Nonetheless, Pryor admitted that slavery's destruction, along with the establishment of the sanctity of the Union, was "the greatest gain of the rebellion." By divine providence, the Civil War had ended the "folly of the Southern people," while the "glorious Union had been perpetuated."[75] This speech, commented the *Brooklyn Daily Eagle,* was the "most notable utterance at the reunion." Pryor represented, it continued, a new type of man "who fought for conviction on the Southern side, who believed that under the constitution the right to secede was guaranteed to every State, and who saw—or thought they saw—in the attitude of the National Government a dangerous movement, shaping itself against their State interests." Pryor represented those white southerners who accepted the war's results, "who whine not at all," were "heartily loyal," and who refused "to be treated as if they had played the part of knaves." Reconciliation required an attitude, the *Eagle* argued, in which sectional conflict of interests receded. In particular, reunions of war veterans became important in the process of reconciliation because they tended to stoke the "sense of brotherhood and the broad patriotism" that northern and southern veterans possessed. Testing out these ideas, Pryor found a receptive audience among Yankee veterans. When he told the Elizabeth group that "he had nothing to apologize for" and that "under the same circumstances, before God I should do it again," his words prompted a "stillness" among the group. But when he came to his next point, that sectional reconciliation was essential to the nation's future, Pryor evoked the "loudest, most vociferous applause of the day."[76]

Pryor's speech at Elizabeth attracted the attention of newspapers, including those in the South. The *Georgia Weekly Telegraph* noted that this same Roger A. Pryor had gone to war "very hot" but came out of it "very much chilled." It found his conversion to reconciliation "decidedly disgusting." The *Lynchburg Virginian* reminded readers that, during the secession crisis, Pryor had denounced the newspaper as "submissionists for endeavoring, with our best ability, to avert the conflict." If the war was folly, "we are in no wise responsible for it." Now, so soon after the war's end, he had "deserted the people, upon whom he did so much to bring the dreadful struggle, for the flesh pots of the North." Pryor, said the *Virginian,* did not represent former Confederates and had "no right to speak for them."[77]

For the most part, historians of Civil War memory have said little about Pryor. David W. Blight, an exception to this generalization, identifies him as paving the way toward a reconciliationist version of the past that emphasized common bonds between northern and southern whites and minimized the significance of slavery and emancipation as driving forces behind the war.[78] Yet the case of Pryor also suggests that postwar reconciliation, for him and for others, was far more complicated and diverse than Blight and other historians have suggested. Addressing northern audiences, Pryor proved more willing to renounce secession and less willing to adopt fully white-supremacist ideas, despite his view about slavery. As a southern carpetbagger he embodied the intersectionalism of the Gilded Age and the search for common ground in the aftermath of the war. But what he said about race suggested a pragmatic path for the South that was attuned to northern audiences and more sensitive to their racial views.

Pryor's best-known statement about healing the war's wounds came in May 1877, when he addressed Union veterans of the Grand Army of the Republic (GAR) during Decoration Day at the Brooklyn Academy of Music. Decoration Day, held every May 30, became a holiday soon after the end of the Civil War to honor the dead; by 1868, it had become a national event. The Philadelphia Centennial Exposition in 1876 helped spur a popular desire to turn the page on the Civil War. In the presidential election of 1876, Democrat Samuel Tilden won the popular vote over Republican Rutherford B. Hayes. But the results were contested because of widespread violence and fraud in three southern states still under military occupation. In January 1877, Congress created a special electoral commission to resolve the dispute, and the so-called Compromise of 1877 awarded Hayes the victory in exchange for the end of occupation in the South. Northern withdrawal from the South fostered a dialogue about what national reunion meant.

The memorializations in New York during Decoration Day 1877 far exceeded anything that had ever occurred in any northern city. George Washington's monument at Union Square was adorned with potted plants along with hundreds of flowering daisies and geraniums around the pedestal, while the statue's head bore a laurel wreath and its outstretched arm a large bouquet. But the Abraham Lincoln statue, which was dedicated only seven years earlier, was "more elaborately ornamented" than any other in the city. Its stone base had lacework of evergreens, with leaves, wisteria sprays, and spirea intertwined. Four baskets contained tropical plants, begonias, and ivy. The panels around the statue had white stars of carnations, with pink roses. Lincoln's head, too, was adorned with a laurel wreath.

The city's Decoration Day events included an elaborate procession, headed by Medal of Honor winner Brig. Gen. Alexander Shaler, that marched past a reviewing stand with the mayor, aldermen, and other city officials. "A great multitude" assembled at Union Square watched, meanwhile, as Broadway was filled with spectators from Fourteenth Street to the Battery, and the procession moved to cemeteries containing Union war dead. In Brooklyn, Green-Wood cemetery, which contained many soldiers' graves, became a center of commemoration. That evening the Brooklyn Academy of Music, one of the largest venues in the area, provided a setting for an audience of 1,000 to hear addresses.

According to the *New York Tribune,* the celebration was "unusually impressive in this city" along with the rest of the country, and the proceedings indicated a universal "spirit of reconciliation and peace." In Chattanooga and other cities in the South, graves of Union and Confederate soldiers were "treated with equal honor." In New York City, the event was preceded by events at Manhattan's two centers of public life, Union and Madison Squares.

Across New York harbor, Brooklyn's Decoration Day began with exercises at Fort Greene, while later a procession adorned soldiers' graves with flowers at Green-Wood Cemetery. The event culminated that evening with Pryor as the featured speaker at the Brooklyn Academy. The stage was filled with dignitaries that included Brooklyn's mayor and some of its aldermen. Joseph Neilson, a chief judge of the city court, presided. Audience boxes were adorned with large American flags and red, white, and blue bunting. Music came from the 13th Regiment band and a children's choir from the Brooklyn Orphan Asylum. The event attracted a comparatively small audience that half-filled the building, but the low attendance may have resulted from a twenty-five-cent admission fee, which went to the establishment of a new soldiers' home in Bath, New York.

Twelve years after the Civil War ended, the GAR leadership at the Brooklyn meeting extended peace feelers to Confederate veterans, 150 of whom agreed to participate. Most controversial was the selection of Pryor as featured speaker. There had been some grumbling during April, when the Barbara Freitchie Post, one of seven GAR posts in Brooklyn, requested that the invitation to the former Confederate general be reconsidered. The dissenters even threatened to boycott the event. When he heard this, Pryor offered to withdraw. But GAR leaders prevailed on him to participate, and he was greeted by "hearty and prolonged" applause. Preparations for the event were afoot, according to the *Brooklyn Daily Eagle,* but the organization's previous "dissensions" had dissipated.[79] In order to emphasize the intersectional nature of the event, the organizing committee also hosted a shorter address by former Union general Isaac S. Catlin.[80]

The meeting's theme was sectional reconciliation. Neilson, who presided, urged that the "people of each State" should express "brotherly kindness" to each other. Former Confederates, he said, wanted to participate in honoring the dead. Pryor, the event's main speaker, next addressed the audience. Expanding on the theme of reconciliation, he made a case for healing the war's wounds. Asserting a theme that became standard among reconciliationists, Pryor claimed that slavery was less important to southerners than the defense of states' rights in that "irrepressible conflict between the principles of State sovereignty and Federal supremacy." Slavery was "philosophically" the "occasion, not the cause of secession," and few northerners believed that it had caused secession and war; it was no more the point of northerners' "attack than of our defense."

Reducing the importance of slavery as a cause of the war, in other words, could then provide a way of achieving reunion. Praising northerners' willingness to "allow us to unite in the homage," he returned the feelings of "kindness and magnanimity" with "all the warmth of our ardent Southern nature" and a desire for intersectional peace in "our agitated and afflicted land." The Civil War, Pryor explained, was the work of politicians rather than military men—the fact that he was a better politician than soldier seemingly escaped him. Soldiers deserved "no blame" for "that stupendous folly, the war of secession." The "bloody business" of disunion and war came from the politicians. It was these antebellum leaders—presumably including Pryor, though he neglected to mention this—who nullified the Constitution and broke the Missouri Compromise. They revived the "almost extinct embers of the abolition agitation" while they also "lashed the popular mind into fury over imaginary wrongs." Soldiers, in contrast, favored conciliation. Although slavery figured in as a cause of the war, conceded Pryor, what truly divided the country was southerners' devotion to states' rights and northerners' dedication to the Union. Each side was, in other words, "impelled by a motive of genuine patriotism, each contending for a cause which shone clear to his conscience, each striving after an object deemed worthy of heroic effort and heroic sacrifice."

Pryor reviewed the "charities of humanity"—the good feeling that soldiers and veterans from both sides possessed—that arose during the war as evidence of improving intersectional feeling. At Appomattox, Grant spared Lee "the humiliations of defeat, and to him and his vanquished veterans accorded the tribute of glory due to a frustrated but heroic struggle." Gen. Joseph Johnston's surrender to Sherman in North Carolina similarly exhibited an "act of intrepid generosity" in which the Yankee general conquered "the affections of his foe, and transformed an embattled host into a community of grateful citizens." Although Secretary of War Stanton invalidated that surrender, "its benign spirit informed and actuated all subsequent policies of reconstruction."

With the formal end to Reconstruction, Pryor offered views—only several months after Hayes's inauguration—that were critical of northern occupation. Repeating the now-common narrative of evil carpetbaggers and compliant freed people, he affirmed that a major obstacle to reunion was Reconstruction—more broadly, any northern interventions in the South. Under military rule, a "patronage of bayonets" violated self-government and imposed a "repulsive compound of alien rule and Federal domination" in which the South was "reduced to the impotence of satrapies." Radical Reconstruction, said Pryor, was doomed to an "inevitable and ignominious overthrow." With Reconstruction's end, he continued, true national reconciliation, in which the South was "respected in her sovereignty and every man in his right," became possible. Henceforth, Pryor maintained, the South would only become a "geographical expression." Southerners participated in the creation of the Constitution in 1787, and their "affection for the Union was a sentiment of ancestral pride." Even the Confederacy's creation reflected an "attachment to principles they had been taught to think paramount to the Union itself." With the end of war, white southerners could reassert the "original ascendance in their hearts" of devotion to nation.

As a former Confederate soldier, Pryor paid tribute "to the graves of the fallen heroes of the Union." He declared to his audience of veterans his "solemn assurance" that their fallen comrades had not died in vain. Union dead had saved the Union, and now Yankee veterans' "policy of justice and magnanimity" toward the defeated South had calmed the "hearts of its once furious but now reclaimed and reconciled foes." In the end, Pryor affirmed, Yankee and Rebel veterans belonged to a larger brotherhood. "Even in the tomb," he said in conclusion, "the Federal and Confederate soldiers will prove the friends of peace, and their blended memories serve as a safeguard of the Union." The address met with "loud and continued applause" in the Brooklyn Academy of Music.[81]

Pryor's 1877 Decoration Day oration, despite the half-full audience, was widely celebrated. Northern newspapers welcomed the address and praised all gatherings that included Rebel and Yankee veterans.[82] For white southerners, Pryor's balance of acceptance of defeat with a reassertion of racial home rule rang true. Although some southern newspapers concluded that the "past cannot be compromised" and that "God knows that the south was right," others praised the address and the concept of sectional reconciliation.[83] The *Nashville Daily American* pointed out that blaming secession and war on the politicians meant that Pryor was "chief among those denounced by himself." When "an old politician begins to denounce politicians," it concluded, "he has not declared the truth."[84] The *Wilmington Morning Star* called it a "quite remarkable" address that was "very brilliant and very eloquent." It praised the rhetoric as "logic on fire" that included a "magnificent sweep in sentences, and high and patriotic thought throughout." Few could match Pryor's "lofty thought and impassioned eloquence," which engendered a "feeling of pride that this master of speech is a Southron." The "universal impression," wrote another contemporary, was that the address had had "a fine effect in correcting Northern sentiment in relation to the conduct of Confederates."[85] As Pryor informed his audience, white southerners wanted white northerners to believe they fought with honor for an honorable cause.

Pryor's prominence as a southern expatriate helped perpetuate his drive for fame and renown. The best example of any fire-eater who so strongly advocated reconciliation, he adapted his message with the changing circumstances. His first statement on reconciliation, the 1867 letter to the *Richmond Whig*, emphasized white southerners' acceptance of defeat and promised a national reintegration that would heal division and bitterness. He suggested that race was key to reconciliation, though his first statements about it proposed, to an unusual degree, a consideration of the status of Black people. Adapting to a changing national mood and political circumstances, he said less about the protection of ex-slaves and more about healing among white people, North and South. Proceeding practically, he tailored his message primarily for a northern white audience that saw the need to protect African Americans during the 1860s but was less concerned after the end of Reconstruction.

Pryor's speaking style, delivered with the same emphasis on performance, sought recognition and fame, though under a different guise. He also continued to depend on newspaper exposure. The *Utica Observer,* accepting his new image, reflected on this transformation. As a young man, Pryor had gained distinction as a hot-headed journalist and politician. Entering the war, he had recreated himself into a soldier. When the war ended, however, he "wasted no time in idle regrets." With considerable hyperbole, the newspaper painted his exile favorably. By moving to New York City, it asserted, Pryor experienced "years of unrequited toil and poverty." But out of this "school of adversity," he "developed the noblest attributes of manhood" as "his wisdom ripened" and his "powers increased." If the Roger Pryor of the late 1850s was drowning "in the sea of troubles which engulphed him," his post–Civil War reincarnation saw the emergence of "a calm, sedate, judicial mind, a tolerant man, a worker, a thinker—the Pryor of 1877."[86] Others noticed that his speech marked both a personal transfiguration and a possible breakthrough in sectional harmony. A correspondent writing from New York in June 1877 observed that Pryor, the former secessionist fire-eater who was the "most active at the opening of the rebellion," might now be regarded as a "representative man." A transplanted southerner in New York, he delivered a speech that marked an "era in our national history which shall be but the beginning of a blessed and a lasting peace." The correspondent left the speech "with most glorious and patriotic associations."[87] Noting Pryor's growing public presence, the *Savannah Morning News* described him as a "wonderful man" who could not, however, "be called handsome." In the lines of his face, one could "almost distinguish the struggle which created this nation."[88]

Over the years Pryor continued to shape his image. Subsequently, he wandered in and out of veteran reunions during the nineteenth century's last decades—and influenced how the Civil War should be remembered.[89] After Grant's death in July 1885, Pryor sponsored a resolution to the New York Democratic Party's convention that praised the former president as an "inflexible patriot and invincible soldier" whose "fitting crown and consummation" was his "dying invocation of peace and good will between the heroes he led and the heroes he conquered."[90] In April 1893, at the celebration of Grant's seventy-fifth birthday, Pryor elaborated on this admiring description. Even more important than his battlefield victories, he told a crowd at the Waldorf Hotel in New York, was Grant's "magnanimity," in which he had "disdained the trophies of victory" and offered a "helping hand to his fallen foe." Grant, Pryor said, was "as great in peace as in war."[91]

In April 1911, Americans recognized the fiftieth anniversary of the bombardment of Fort Sumter. From New York, Pryor, now eighty-three, described himself as the sole survivor of the event and commemorated the anniversary with other veterans. Newspapers recalled his fiery speech at Charleston's Mills House, in which Pryor promised to persuade Virginia to adopt immediate secession.[92] He encouraged the characterization of himself as the "sole survivor" of Fort Sumter at this time. More accurately, Pryor might have been the last person to witness the Confederates' initial barrage. The attack had more meaning for him, according to one newspaper account, than it would "for no other man alive." Recalling his role as an incendiary secessionist, Pryor described how his rhetoric encouraging violence began a shooting war and drew Upper South states like Virginia into the Confederacy. Disunion, he maintained, was "what we had been seeking during all the exciting days of that winter—something that would swing the border states into line. It needed only the striking of one blow." He added, "When that came at Sumter the result was precisely as we had foreseen."[93]

Roger A. Pryor late in life.
Library of Congress, Washington, DC.

A half century after the onset of the war, Pryor remained a central figure. An ardent secessionist, he had preached a fiery rhetoric of disunion. Yet accounts of the aging ex-Confederate emphasized a different persona, cemented by decades of his experience as an advocate of postwar reconciliation. No longer addressed as "General," he was now known as "Judge." Where the young fire-eater hothead was impulsive and obsessed with personal honor, the older jurist had become "one of the gentlest, kindliest of men." One newspaperman found that, though the old general in his dotage was "delightful in some of his personal reminiscences," he now preferred not speak about the "more active and exciting incidents of the early days of the Civil War"; he apparently believed that it was better that future historians tell the story.[94] The occasion was observed in the national press. The results of a shooting war, observed the *Charleston News & Courier,* reinforced the South's faith in "justness of the cause for whose achievement we have suffered obloquy and flared perils of vast magnitude." The war involved divine sanction; God's hand "guided and defended us all through the momentous conflict." It further declared, "We call the roll of those engaged in the battle and each soldier is here to answer to his name," adding that "no tombstone will throw its shadow upon that bright triumphant day."[95]

In later life, while Sara published several novels and two memoirs that trumpeted the reconciliationist version of the past, Roger became a judge in the court of common pleas in 1889 and, beginning six years later, occupied a seat on the state supreme court for a decade. These judicial appointments, according to newspaper accounts, resulted from bribes to Tammany. During the mayoral campaign in 1897, Henry George claimed that Pryor paid $35,000 for his judgeship.[96]

In 1899, Roger Pryor retired and largely withdrew from public life. In 1910, when he and Sara celebrated sixty years of marriage, more than a thousand people attended a reception in their honor.[97] Sara died on February 15, 1912; Roger's death followed on March 14, 1919, at age ninety. Describing his careers as secessionist and Confederate general, the *Atlanta Constitution* eulogized him as a "journalist-soldier-jurist." "I cannot forget the civil war," he told an interviewer during his last days. "But in generations to come people will think of those differences less and less. . . . The words north and south are simply geographical expressions now, and have no political significance whatever." For him, the "simple word 'union' expresses everything."[98]

ACKNOWLEDGMENTS

In the course of delivering the Fleming Lectures at LSU and turning those into a book, I have imposed on the generosity of a number of people. I delivered the lectures in an online format, amid the peak of a global pandemic. Originally scheduled to occur in March 2020, the lectures were postponed for almost eight months. In the end, however, COVID-19 proved unable to stop either my enthusiasm or that of the audience.

I am very grateful especially to Victor Stater of the LSU History Department for issuing the invitation to deliver these lectures. Aaron Sheehan-Dean proved a superb host, and he both performed the administrative duties and provided the intellectual enthusiasm to make these musings into what I hope was a success. I am particularly grateful to those scholars who read all or portions of the manuscript in various forms: Jim Broomall, Peter Carmichael, Susanna Lee, Aaron Sheehan-Dean, and Angie Zombek. Aurélia Aubert provided a close reading, as did Brenda Withington. The advice of all these scholars proved essential in improving the intellectual structure of the book, and they helped me navigate the treacherous waters of Civil War history. Given that the lectures were written during the worst period of the pandemic, I greatly appreciated support from librarians across the country: Matthew Guillen and Andrew Foster of the Virginia Museum of History and Culture; Grace Hale of Albert and Shirley Small Special Collections, University of Virginia Library; and Mel Frizzell, Special Collections Assistant, Old Dominion Library.

Rand Dotson of the LSU Press has been a wonderful editor, and I appreciate his efficiency and persistence in seeing this book to completion. In addition, Kevin Brock and Neal Novak skillfully edited the manuscript. As always, I have relied on the careful editing and clear thinking of Susannah Link.

NOTES

Introduction

1. According to Pryor's wife, Sara Rice Pryor, their correspondence was lost in the turmoil of 1865. At the same time, there is no evidence of surviving correspondence thereafter. Sara Agnes Rice Pryor, *My Day: Reminiscences of a Long Life* (New York: Macmillan, 1909), 110.

2. Robert S. Holzman, *Adapt or Perish: The Life of General Roger A. Pryor, C.S.A.* (Hamden, CT: Archon Books, 1976); John C. Waugh, *Surviving the Confederacy: Rebellion, Ruin, and Recovery—Roger and Sara Pryor during the Civil War* (New York: Harcourt, 2002). Also see Thomas P. Wilsted, "Roger A. Pryor: Secessionist and Soldier, 1849–1865" (MA thesis, University of Wisconsin, 1968).

3. John C. Parker, "Jane White's Comments about Gen. Roger Pryor," February 9, 1957, Accession 5550, University of Virginia Library, Charlottesville.

4. Stephen W. Berry II, *All That Makes a Man: Love and Ambition in the Civil War South* (New York: Oxford University Press, 2003), 11, 19–20.

5. Amy Greenberg, *Manifest Manhood and the Antebellum Empire* (Cambridge: Cambridge University Press, 2005), 11–12, 271 (quote, 12).

6. Kenneth S. Greenberg, *Masters and Statesmen: The Political Culture of American Slavery* (Baltimore: Johns Hopkins University Press, 1985), 16.

7. Walter Allen Watson, *Notes on Southside Virginia* (Richmond: Superintendent of Public Printing, 1925), 177–78.

8. Quoted in Wilsted, "Roger A. Pryor," 50.

9. *Daily National Democrat (Marysville, CA),* January 8, 1860.

10. John Herbert Claiborne, *Seventy-Five Years in Old Virginia* (New York: Neale, 1904), 91–92; Pryor, *My Day,* 127.

11. Parker, "Jane White's Comments about Gen. Roger Pryor," University of Virginia Library.

12. *Monroe (LA) Register*, January 5, 1860.

13. "John W. Noell and Roger A. Pryor," *White Cloud (KS) Chief*, February 23, 1860.

14. Claiborne, *Seventy-Five Years in Old Virginia*, 91–92; Pryor, *My Day*, 127.

15. Quoted in *Alexandria (VA) Gazette*, February 4, 1860.

16. "Mr. Pryor upon Brute Force," *National Republican (Washington, DC)*, March 19, 1861.

17. James J. Broomall, *Private Confederacies: The Emotional Worlds of Southern Men as Citizens and Soldiers* (Chapel Hill: University of North Carolina Press, 2019); Diane Miller Sommerville, *Aberration of Mind: Suicide and Suffering in the Civil War–Era South* (Chapel Hill: University of North Carolina Press, 2018); Peter S. Carmichael, *The War for the Common Soldier: How Men Thought, Fought, and Survived in Civil War Armies* (Chapel Hill: University of North Carolina Press, 2018).

18. *New York Mail*, quoted in *Portland (ME) Daily Press*, October 5, 1867.

19. LeeAnn Whites, *The Civil War as a Crisis in Gender: Augusta, Georgia, 1860–1890* (Athens: University of Georgia Press, 2000); Phillip S. Paludan, "The American Civil War Considered as a Crisis in Law and Order," *American Historical Review* 77 (October 1972): 1013–34.

20. Quoted in Samuel T. McSeveney, "Revenge for the Carpetbaggers: A Note on Ex-Confederates in New York City Politics after the Civil War," *New York History* 73 (January 1992): 40.

21. T. C. Evans, "Former Judge Roger A. Pryor Discusses Some Questions of the Hour," *New York Times*, February 4, 1906.

1. A Champion of the South

1. Owen Lovejoy, *The Barbarism of Slavery: Speech of Hon. Owen Lovejoy Delivered in the House of Representatives, April 5, 1860* (n.p., 1860); *Richmond Enquirer*, April 10, 1860.

2. *Congressional Globe*, April 11, 1860.

3. Kenneth S. Greenberg, "The Nose, the Lie, and the Duel in the Antebellum South," *American Historical Review* 95 (February 1990): 57–58. For an attempt to quantify dueling, see Matthew Byron, "Crime and Punishment: The Impotency of Dueling Laws in the United States" (PhD diss., University of Arkansas, 2008).

4. James J. Broomall, "Wartime Masculinities," in *The Cambridge History of the American Civil War*, ed. Aaron Sheehan-Dean, 3 vols. (Cambridge: Cambridge University Press, 2019), 3:3–4. See also Broomall, *Private Confederacies*.

5. Reid Mitchell, *The Vacant Chair: The Northern Soldier Leaves Home* (New York: Oxford University Press, 1995), 11–12.

6. *Richmond Enquirer,* June 4, 1852. Pryor became better known in party circles after he supported a resolution affirming the new fugitive slave law that was passed as part of the Compromise of 1850. The national government's duty, the resolution read, was to enforce the law. All attempts to "impair its efficacy or weaken its guarantee" should be opposed by "every well-wisher of the Republic." *Richmond Enquirer,* June 8, 1852.

7. See *Proceedings of the Democratic National Convention, Held at Baltimore, June 1–5, 1852, for the Nomination of Candidates for President and Vice President of the United States* (Baltimore: Democratic National Convention, 1852).

8. *Fayetteville North-Carolinian,* September 11, 1852.

9. Holzman, *Adapt or Perish,* 15–16.

10. *Richmond Enquirer,* January 4, 1853; Pryor, *My Day,* 84, 90, 100–101; Sara Agnes Rice Pryor, *Reminiscences of Peace and War* (New York: Macmillan, 1904), 15; Holzman, *Adapt or Perish,* 16–17.

11. *Washington National Era,* June 2, 1853.

12. Holzman, *Adapt or Perish,* 17.

13. "Russia and the United States," *New York Daily Tribune,* June 2, 1853.

14. "'Out, Damned Spot!'" *Washington Republic,* June 7, 1853.

15. *Richmond Enquirer,* December 21, 1855. For the fullest discussion of Pryor's diplomatic mission, see Wilsted, "Roger A. Pryor," 20–26.

16. Pryor, *My Day,* 111.

17. The *Enquirer*'s editors predicted that Pryor would provide "new energy and spirit" that would energize the "Democracy in all portions of the country." *Richmond Enquirer,* August 12, 1853.

18. *Washington Union,* March 10, 1857.

19. Pryor, *My Day,* 125–26.

20. "The Difficulty," *Daily Southern Argus (Norfolk VA),* October 2, 1852.

21. Quoted in Tim Talbott, "O. Jennings Wise: Editor, Duelist, Soldier, Southerner, *Random Thoughts on History* (blog), January 9, 2017, http://randomthoughtsonhistory.blogspot.com/2017/01/o-jennings-wise-editor-duelist-soldier.html.

22. Jennings Wise to Henry A. Wise, July 12, 1851, Wise Family Papers, Virginia Historical Society, Richmond. William Lamb subsequently described Bayly as a "drunken puppy." Diary of William Lamb, April 30, 1855, Manuscripts and Rare Books Department, Swem Library, College of William and Mary, Williamsburg, VA.

23. Virginius Dabney, *Richmond: The Story of a City* (Charlottesville: University Press of Virginia, 1990), 132.

24. For Wise's version of events, see "A Card," January 24, 1858, *Richmond Enquirer,* January 26, 1858. See also R. Ridgway to the public, ibid.; R. Ridgway to O. Jennings Wise, January 23, 1858, ibid.; and Wise to Ridgway, January 23, 1858, ibid.

25. John Young Mason to Roscoe Briggs Heath, April 21, 1858, Mason Family Papers, Virginia Historical Society, Richmond; *Wytheville (VA) Times,* September 25, 1858; Charles H.

Ambler, *Sectionalism in Virginia from 1776 to 1861* (Chicago: University of Chicago Press, 1910), 321–22; Craig M. Simpson, *A Good Southerner: The Life of Henry A. Wise of Virginia (Chapel Hill: University of North Carolina Press, 1985),* 178–79. Details of the duel are provided in *New York Times,* September 24, 1858; C. Irving, "A Card," September 18, 1858, *Wytheville (VA) Times,* October 2, 1858; and "Duel near Richmond" and "A Duel," *Petersburg Daily Express,* September 18, 1858. On the legal aftermath of this duel, see "Legal Enquiry into the Alleged Duel," *Richmond Enquirer,* September 21, 1858; and "The Duel Investigating Court," ibid., September 24, 1858; Patrick Henry Aylett, *Virginia Index* (Richmond), July 19, 1859; Aylett, "A Card," reprinted from the *Richmond Examiner* in ibid., August 3, 1859.

26. Bertram Wyatt-Brown, *Southern Honor: Ethics & Behavior in the Old South* (New York: Oxford University Press, 1982), xv.

27. See, for example, "Young Man's Friend" and "Some Remarks on Duelling," *Alexandria Gazette and Virginia Advertiser,* August 4, 1856. For the best study of gender and politics in Virginia, see Elizabeth R. Varon, *We Mean to Be Counted: White Women and Politics in Antebellum Virginia* (Chapel Hill: University of North Carolina Press, 1998). On honor, see Wyatt-Brown, *Southern Honor.* On duels, see Greenberg, *Masters and Statesmen,* 23–44; and Dickson Bruce Jr., *Violence and Culture in the Antebellum South* (Austin: University of Texas Press, 1979), 21–43.

28. Watson, *Notes on Southside Virginia,* 176.

29. Bertram Wyatt-Brown, "Andrew Jackson's Honor," *Journal of the Early Republic* 17 (Spring 1997): 35.

30. *Wellsburg (VA) Herald,* May 14, 1858.

31. In January 1810, the Virginia legislature criminalized "the barbarous custom of dueling" by categorizing any resulting deaths as murder. Anyone issuing or accepting a challenge, in addition, lost political rights of officeholding; public officials took an oath swearing that they had never been involved in a duel. Officers of the law were instructed to prevent duels if they heard of them. *Revised Code of the Laws of Virginia* (Richmond: Thomas Ritchie, 1819), 583–85.

32. *Richmond Enquirer,* December 30, 1859.

33. Duels, writes Kenneth Greenberg, "could never really be private battles; they had to be public." Greenberg, *Masters and Statesmen,* 24, 28, 31.

34. As a *New York Herald* correspondent observed, this new political party represented "an entirely different set of customers" who were "bold, hopeful, defiant—hungry for a fight—regular rough and tumble, pull down and drag out boys." When taunted about "their want of dignity, their secrecy, [and] their underground burrowing," Know-Nothings responded to their opponents with aggressive rhetoric. "Know Something," *New York Herald,* March 17, 1855.

35. "Know Something"; "Virginia Politics," *New York Herald,* March 17, 1855.

36. *Richmond Daily Dispatch,* August 1, 1856.

37. *Richmond Daily Dispatch,* August 1, 1856.

38. Quoted in *Richmond Daily Dispatch,* August 4, 1856.

39. *Washington Star* and *Petersburg Express,* quoted in the *Richmond Daily Dispatch,* August 8, 1856.

40. "Keitt Knocked Down Three Times," *Chicago Tribune,* February 10, 1858.

41. Charles James Faulkner to Alexander R. Boteler, June 2, July 9, 20, August 8, 1855, box 1, Alexander R. Boteler Papers, Duke University Library, Durham, NC; Boteler to Faulkner, June 20, July 12, August 2, ibid.; James Stewart to Faulkner, July 2, 1855, copy, ibid. On Bedinger, see entry in John T. Kneebone et al., eds., *Dictionary of Virginia Biography,* 3 vols. (Richmond: Library of Virginia, 1998–2006), 1:432–33.

42. G. H. Meade to B., August 20, 1855, box 1, Boteler Papers; Strother to Boteler, August 24, 1855, ibid.; A. J. Bidball to David H. Strother, September 4, 7, 1855, ibid.; Strother to Boteler, September 7, October 2, 17, 19, 28, 1855, ibid.; Boteler to Strother, September 17, October 19, 29, 26, 20, 1855, ibid.; Faulkner to Strother, October 17, 1855, ibid.; David Strother and H. B. Tyler, statement, October 23, 1855, ibid.

43. Strother to Boteler, September 15, 1855, box 1, Boteler Papers. James Lawson Kemper of Madison County, who served as a member of the House of Delegates during the 1850s, became involved in a fracas with Dr. George N. Thrift, who in 1853 accused Kemper of lying during a court case. When Kemper demanded satisfaction, elaborate negotiations followed that led to a compromise, face-saving settlement. See James L. Kemper, *A History of the Late Difficulties in Madison, November 1853* (Washington: Henry Polkinhorn, 1853); and D. H. E. Sanders, statement, June 28, 1852, Papers of George N. Thrift, University of Virginia Library, Charlottesville.

44. "Ex-Governor William Smith," *Richmond Enquirer,* March 15, 1855.

45. See the exchange in "To the People of Virginia," *Richmond Enquirer,* May 22, 1855.

46. *New York Herald,* October 17, 1856.

47. Pryor arrived in Washington on October 5, two days after terms had been settled. Further negotiations about location delayed the duel until October 8, a week after he had issued his original challenge. Pryor to Botts, October 1, 3, 1856; Botts to Pryor, October 3, 1856; F. J. Smith to Pryor, October 3, 1856; and T. P. Chiseman to Botts, October 8, 1856, all in *Washington Union,* October 8, 1856.

48. *Richmond Enquirer,* October 8, 1856; "End of the Duel," *Richmond Daily Dispatch,* October 8, 1855.

49. "Duel Prevented," *Alexandria (VA) Gazette,* October 8, 1856.

50. "End of the Duel," *Richmond Daily Dispatch,* October 8, 1855; *Richmond Enquirer,* October 31, 1856.

51. John Minor Botts to Roger A. Pryor, October 12, 1856, *New York Herald,* October 17, 1856. The episode was recounted twenty-eight years later in the press. See "The Botts Brothers," *San Francisco Daily Evening Dispatch,* October 6, 1884.

52. For the Bennett-Pryor feud, see Waugh, *Surviving the Confederacy,* 59–60.

53. *New York Herald,* October 17, 1856.

54. *Richmond Daily Dispatch,* November 3, 10, 1856.

55. Waugh, *Surviving the Confederacy,* 59.

56. *Richmond Daily Dispatch,* November 3, 1856.

57. *Richmond Daily Dispatch,* November 8, 1856.

58. *Richmond Daily Dispatch,* November 10, 1856.

59. *Richmond Daily Dispatch,* November 11, 1856.

60. *Richmond Daily Dispatch,* November 13, 14, 1856.

61. *Richmond Daily Dispatch,* February 13, 1857.

62. *Richmond Daily Dispatch,* November 17, 1856.

63. Quoted in Pryor, *My Day,* 129–30.

64. *Richmond Times-Dispatch,* November 2, 1902, quoted in Pryor, *My Day,* 30.

65. Pryor to the editor, May 3, 1859, *Richmond Enquirer,* May 6, 1859. See also Michael Woods, *Arguing until Doomsday: Stephen Douglas, Jefferson Davis, and the Struggle for American Democracy* (Chapel Hill: University of North Carolina Press, 2020).

66. Quoted in Pryor, *My Day,* 128–29.

67. Quoted in Pryor, *My Day,* 129–30.

68. "Mr. Pryor—Canvass in the Fourth Congressional District," *Richmond Enquirer,* October 18, 1859.

69. "Fourth Congressional District," *Richmond Enquirer,* October 21, 1859.

70. Pryor, *Reminiscences,* 138.

71. Pryor, *Reminiscences,* 42.

72. Pryor, *My Day,* 39.

73. Eric H. Walther, *The Fire-Eaters* (Baton Rouge: Louisiana State University Press, 1992). Peter S. Carmichael describes a younger group of southern radicals in *The Last Generation: Young Virginians in Peace, War, and Reunion* (Chapel Hill: University of North Carolina Press, 2005).

74. Ulrich Bonnell Phillips, *The Course of the South to Secession* (New York, 1939), 128.

75. Joanne B. Freeman, *Field of Blood: Violence in Congress and the Road to Civil War* (New York: Macmillan, 2018).

76. *Principles and Policy of the Black Republican Party* (Washington: Congressional Globe Office, 1859).

77. Ollinger Crenshaw, "The Speakership Contest of 1859–1860: John Sherman's Election a Cause of Disruption?," *Mississippi Valley Historical Review* 29 (December 1942): 323–38; Ben A. Riley, "The Pryor-Potter Affair: Nineteenth Century Civilian Conflict as Precursor to Civil War," *Journal of the West Virginia Historical Association* 8 (Spring 1984): 29.

78. *Congressional Globe,* January 17, 1860, 492.

79. *New York Herald,* January 13, 1860.

80. "The Struggle in the House of Representatives," *New York Herald,* January 19, 1860.

81. *Congressional Globe,* January 20, 1860, 540.

82. *New York Daily Tribune,* April 13, 1860.

83. "The Case of Messrs. Potter and Pryor," *New York Daily Tribune,* April 13, 1860.

84. *New York Daily Tribune,* April 12, 1860; "The Potter and Pryor Affair," *New York Herald,* April 16, 1860; "The Late Gen. Lander," *Wheeling (VA) Daily Intelligencer,* March 5, 1862; Riley, "Pryor-Potter Affair," 34. On Lander, see Gary L. Ecelbarger, *Frederick W. Lander: The Great Natural American Soldier* (Baton Rouge: Louisiana State University Press, 2000).

85. "The Congressional Election—Col. Roger A. Pryor," *Richmond Enquirer,* October 11, 1861.

86. "The Opera Excitement on the Rise," *New York Herald,* April 23, 1860.

87. "Spirit of the Morning Press," *Washington Evening Star,* March 19, 1861.

88. "Our Washington Correspondence," *New York Herald,* April 16, 1860; "Virginia," *Green Mountain Freeman (Montpelier, VT),* April 18, 1861.

89. *New York Daily Tribune,* April 13, 1860; Riley, "Pryor-Potter Affair," 35.

90. "The Case of Messrs. Potter and Pryor," *New York Daily Tribune,* April 13, 1860; "The Pryor and Potter Difficulty," *New York Herald,* April 17, 1860.

91. *New York Daily Tribune,* April 18, 1860.

92. "What the Rebels Say of Copperheads," *New Haven (CT) Palladium,* January 26, 1864.

93. "Southern Sentiment vs. Southern Abuse of the *New York Herald,*" *New York Daily Herald,* January 23, 1858.

94. Carmichael, *Last Generation.*

95. Pryor to the editor, December 20, 1860, *Richmond Enquirer,* December 25, 1860.

96. *Alexandria (VA) Gazette,* June 26, 1876.

97. After Potter's family donated the knife to Lawrence University, the school transferred it to the Wisconsin Historical Society in 1957. *Chattanooga Daily Times,* December 15, 1882, January 29 1892; "'Bowie Knife' Potter Dead," *Indianapolis Journal,* May 19, 1889. For an explanation of the knife's fate, see "The 'Monster Knife' of John Fox Potter," Wisconsin Historical Society, April 7, 2005, https://www.wisconsinhistory.org/Records/Article/CS2802.

2. The Chevalier of the Appomattox

1. "The Capture of Roger A. Pryor," *New York Herald,* December 3, 1864, in *Richmond Examiner,* November 30, 1864.

2. "The Army of the Potomac," *New York Times,* December 4, 1864.

3. Henry S. Burrage to Robert E. Lee, November 8, 1864, in *War Papers Read before the Commandery of the State of Maine,* 4 vols. (Portland, ME: Lefavor-Tower, 1898–1915), 4:171–72.

4. "Grand Democratic Rally," *Richmond Enquirer,* September 4, 1860.

5. *Georgia Weekly Telegraph (Macon),* September 27, 1860; "Was Warned of Death," *Chicago Daily Tribune,* February 7, 1909.

6. Pryor to William J. Cheatham, December 20, 1860, *New Bern (NC) Weekly Progress,* December 28, 1860.

7. *Abbeville (SC) Press,* January 4, 1861.

8. *Petersburg Express,* March 12, 1861, quoted in "Secession Meeting," *Richmond Enquirer,* March 14, 1861.

9. "Exciting Scene in Virginia Church," *Delaware State Journal and Statesman (Wilmington),* January 22, 1861.

10. *Richmond Daily Dispatch,* March 16, 1861.

11. Watson, *Notes on Southside Virginia,* 177–78; "Letter from Richmond," *Alexandria (VA) Gazette,* March 19, 1861; "Mr. Pryor on Brute Force," *National Republican (Washington, DC),* March 19, 1861; Holzman, *Adapt or Perish,* 52–53; "The Political Cauldron," *Wheeling (VA) Daily Intelligencer,* March 20, 1861.

12. *Richmond Daily Dispatch,* April 4, 1861; *Washington Evening Star,* April 5, 1861. See also *Alexandria (VA) Gazette,* March 29, April 9, 1861.

13. "Enthusiastic Meeting in Brunswick," *Memphis Daily Appeal,* March 30, 1861.

14. *Richmond Enquirer,* April 11, 1861.

15. Mary Boykin Chesnut, *A Diary from Dixie* (New York: D. Appleton, 1914), 37.

16. Pryor, *Reminiscences,* 120–21.

17. Pryor, *My Day,* 158–59; *Richmond Daily Dispatch,* April 13, 1861; *Atlanta Southern Confederacy,* April 13, 1861 (emphasis original).

18. *Richmond Enquirer,* semiweekly ed., April 13, 1861; *National Republican (Washington, DC),* April 13, 1861; William E. Dodd, *Statesmen of the Old South: From Radicalism to Conservative Revolt* (New York: Macmillan, 1911), 220–21.

19. "A Hard Story on Pryor," *Macon (GA) Daily Telegraph,* April 27, 1861; *Washington Evening Star,* April 23, 1861.

20. Apparently, this was based on a conversation with Dodd on December 30, 1909. Dodd, *Statesmen of the Old South,* 221. Also see Clement A. Evans et al., *Confederate Military History: A Library of Confederate States History,* 12 vols. (Atlanta: Confederate Publishing, 1899), 4: 654.

21. *New York Herald,* April 19, 1861; "The Secession of Virginia," *Richmond Dispatch,* April 20, 1861.

22. *Richmond Daily Dispatch,* April 26, 27, 1861.

23. Pryor, speech, May 10, 1858, "Proceedings of the Southern Convention at Montgomery, Alabama," *De Bow's Review* 24, no. 6 (June 1858): 574–606; "Hon. William L. Yancey and Roger A. Pryor," *Richmond Enquirer,* October 5, 1858. For a fuller discussion, see Harvey Wish, "The Revival of the African Slave Trade in the United States, 1856–1860," *Mississippi Valley Historical Review* 27 (March 1941): 569–88; and Walther, *Fire-Eaters,* 69–70.

24. *Richmond Daily Dispatch,* May 29, 1861.

25. Although Pryor served in both the Provisional Confederate Congress and the permanent Congress, in April 1862 Congress prohibited Confederate officers from occupying political office. Waugh, *Surviving the Confederacy,* 134.

26. *Richmond Daily Dispatch,* April 19, 23, August 14, 1861, April 7, 1862; Waugh, *Surviving the Confederacy,* 109–10.

27. *Richmond Daily Dispatch,* November 22, 1861.

28. Lee A. Wallace Jr., *3rd Virginia Infantry* (Lynchburg, VA: H. E. Howard, 1986), 10. During the summer of 1861, Pryor attempted to crack down on drinking in his regiment. Wilsted, "Roger A. Pryor," 97–98. According to Sara, the troops' discontent resulted from Pryor's efforts to ban alcohol in order to reduce drunkenness. Pryor, *My Day,* 165.

29. Waugh, *Surviving the Confederacy,* 125, 137.

30. Wilsted, "Roger A. Pryor," 98–99.

31. D. Scott Hartwig, *To Antietam Creek: The Maryland Campaign of September 1862* (Baltimore: Johns Hopkins University Press, 2012), 77.

32. Waugh, *Surviving the Confederacy,* 139; Wallace, *3rd Virginia Infantry,* 23. For an example of the pro-Pryor lobbying campaign, see also Thomas S. Bocock et al. to Jefferson Davis, December 4, 1861; and William Mahone to S. Bassett French, December 18, 1861, Roger A. Pryor, compiled service record, fold3.com.

33. Pryor, *My Day,* 167–68; *Richmond Daily Dispatch,* July 26, 1861, June 5, 28, 1862.

34. "Pryor's Brigade," *Richmond Dispatch,* May 20, 1862.

35. Robert H. Miller to his father, July 23, 1862, in Forrest P. Connor, ed., "Letters of Lieutenant Robert H. Miller to His Family, 1861–1862," *Virginia Magazine of History and Biography* 70 (January 1962): 87.

36. Joseph T. Glatthaar, *General Lee's Army: From Victory to Collapse* (New York: Free Press, 2008), 192.

37. *Charleston Daily Courier,* September 11, 1862; *Richmond Daily Dispatch,* September 9, 26, 1862.

38. *Wisconsin State Journal (Madison),* September 8, 1862.

39. *Richmond Daily Dispatch,* September 28, 1862.

40. "Roger A. Pryor," *Philadelphia Evening Telegraph,* December 2, 1867.

41. Accounts in northern newspapers, which also widely covered the incident, claimed that Pryor had escaped by shooting his captor with a hidden Derringer pistol. See, for example, *Wisconsin State Journal (Madison),* September 8, 1862.

42. E. D. Donnelly to Andrew Johnson, September 19, 1865; and Donnelly to Edwin Staunton, November 15, 1865, Roger A. Pryor file, Confederate Amnesty Papers, fold3.com. Although his letter arrived after Pryor obtained a pardon, Donnelly did not permit the matter to rest there. In November 1867, he wrote a long letter to the *Pittsburgh Commercial.* "Who that has travelled over the sanguinary fields of slaughter from Me-

chanicsville to Malvern Hill," the newspaper maintained in response, "has not seen the stripped bodies of our men, stabbed, wantonly stabbed, by the passing Rebel soldiery? Or the gash of some chivalric Rebel officer's virgin sword in the lair skin of his dead enemy?" "Bayonet and Sabre Wounds—A Chivalric Act of Roger A. Pryor," *Pittsburgh Commercial,* November 26, 1867.

43. Parker, "Jane White's Comments about Gen. Roger Pryor," University of Virginia Library.

44. Waugh, *Surviving the Confederacy,* 167; *Winona (MN) Daily Republican,* September 27, 1862; Wallace, *3rd Virginia Infantry,* 31; Robert K. Krick, "The Army of Northern Virginia: Its Circumstances, Its Opportunities, and Why It Should Not Have Been at Sharpsburg," in *Antietam: Essays on the 1862 Maryland Campaign,* ed. Gary Gallagher (Kent, OH: Kent State University Press, 1989), 48. On September 29, 1862, the *National Republican* reported casualties of 1,652 out of a force of 2,200 men, losses of about three-fifths.

45. Joseph Pierrto, ed., *The Maryland Campaign of September 1962: Ezra Carman's Definitive Study of the Union and Confederate Armies at Antietam* (New York: Routledge, 2008), 286.

46. Douglas Southall Freeman, *Lee's Lieutenants: A Study in Command,* abridged ed. (New York: Touchstone, 1998), 363; Krick, "Army of Northern Virginia," 48. One contemporary estimated that Pryor's brigade suffered casualties of 1,280 out of 2,200 men. "From Harpers Ferry," *National Republican (Washington, DC),* September 29, 1862.

47. *Richmond Daily Dispatch,* October 1, 1862; Pryor, "The Soldier the Friend of Peace and Union," in Roger A. Pryor, *Essays and Addresses* (New York, Neale Pub. Co., 1912), 63. Sara Pryor described another incident in the aftermath of Antietam that advertised her husband's gallantry. She claimed that during the Meagher-Pryor meeting, another Union officer came forward with a "small bundle," a handkerchief that contained a gold watch, a pair of gold cufflinks, and silver that was looted from a dead Florida soldier. Years later she showed the items, which she kept, to "an aged relative." The woman saw "pin-scratched letters" on the cufflinks, "perfectly plain" initials on the inside of these sleeve buttons. Sara later met a Florida Confederate veteran who recognized the initials and arranged for them to be returned to the dead soldier's family. Pryor, *Reminiscences,* 195.

48. See, for example, *Galveston Daily News,* September 12, 1883.

49. Robert E. Lee to George W. Randolph, November 10, 1862, US War Department, *War of the Rebellion: A Compilation of the Official Records of the Union and Confederate Armies,* ser. 1, 19(2):708–9 (hereafter cited as *OR,* all citations to ser. 1 unless otherwise stated).

50. Lee to Pryor, November 25, 1962, in Pryor, *Reminiscences,* 211.

51. Krick, "Army of Northern Virginia," 48.

52. Waugh, *Surviving the Confederacy,* 171.

53. *Abbeville (SC) Medium,* quoted in *Watchman and Southron* (Sumter, SC), April 10, 1889.

54. Pryor, *My Day,* 179; Pryor, *Reminiscences,* 210–11.

55. "Recollections of Confederate Officers," *Galveston Daily News,* May 16, 1897.

56. Pryor, *Reminiscences,* 211–12; S. G. French, report, March 3, 1863, *OR,* 36:906.

57. Pryor, *Reminiscences,* 230.

58. Pryor to Gustavus W. Smith, January 6, 1863, *OR,* 36:845–46.

59. Pryor, *Reminiscences,* 218; Parker, "Jane White's Comments about Gen. Roger A. Pryor," University of Virginia Library.

60. John J. Peck to H. W. Halleck, January 13, 1863; Peck to John A. Dix, January 13, 1863; and Dix to Peck, January 13, 1863; *OR,* 36:513; Pryor, report, February 4, 1863, ibid., 142–44; Waugh, *Surviving the Confederacy,* 181, 197; Wilsted, "Roger A. Pryor," 118; "Skirmish in Isle of Wight County," *Richmond Daily Dispatch,* December 25, 1862; "The News," *Richmond Enquirer,* February 6, 1863; "The Affair on the Blackwater," *Weekly National Intelligencer (Washington, DC),* January 17, 1863. Sara later described how she joined her husband in the Blackwater region. Pryor, *Reminiscences,* 213–18.

61. G. W. Smith to R. E. Lee, November 12, 1862, *OR,* 19(2):715.

62. Pryor, *Reminiscences,* 239.

63. Watson, *Notes on Southside Virginia,* 176–77.

64. "The North to the War," *Richmond Enquirer,* March 14, 1863; Pryor, *My Day,* 190–92; Waugh, *Surviving the Confederacy,* 198.

65. Seddon to French, October 29, 1863, Pryor, compiled service record, fold3.com.

66. Pryor, *My Day,* 192.

67. "Pneumonia Kills Last Survivor of Ft. Sumter Fight," *Richmond Times-Dispatch,* March 15, 1919.

68. Pryor, *My Day,* 198.

69. Pryor, *My Day,* 192–93.

70. *Richmond Daily Dispatch,* September 30, 1863.

71. "Mr. Pryor in Washington," *New York Times,* November 30, 1864.

72. *Cleveland Morning Leader,* November 30, 1864.

73. Pryor, *Reminiscences,* 288.

74. *Richmond Daily Dispatch,* November 30, 1864; Waugh, *Surviving the Confederacy,* 227.

75. Pryor, *Reminiscences,* 306.

76. Pryor, *My Day,* 206.

77. G. S. Innis to Benjamin F. Butler, August 6, 1864, *OR,* 42(2):72.

78. Civil War Service Records (CMSR)—Confederate—Virginia Third Cavalry (Second Virginia Cavalry), fold3.com.

79. Pryor, *Reminiscences,* 307.

80. "Mr. Pryor in Washington," *New York Times,* November 30, 1864.

81. *Cleveland Morning Leader,* November 20, 1864.

82. "Mr. Pryor in Washington," *New York Times,* November 30, 1864.

83. "Arrival of a Notorious Rebel Prisoner—Roger A. Pryor in Limbo," *San Francisco Daily Bulletin,* December 29, 1864.

84. *New York Herald,* November 30, December 1, 1864, quoted in Roger A. Pryor Jr., *The Capture of Gen. Roger A. Pryor (n.p., 1889),* 10; Pryor, *Reminiscences,* 309–10, 322–23.

85. "Release of Roger A. Pryor," *New York Sun,* February 27, 1865.

86. Holzman, *Adapt or Perish,* 21.

87. Pryor, *My Day,* 207.

88. "Mr. Lincoln and Roger Pryor," *Buchanan County Bulletin,* June 3, 1870; Abraham Lincoln to U. S. Grant, February 24, 1865, and Grant to Lincoln, February 25, 1865, in *Collected Works of Abraham Lincoln,* ed. Roy P. Basler, 9 vols. (New Brunswick, NJ: Rutgers University Press, 1953–55), vol. 8, n. 1; "Pryor and Forney," *Daily Constitutionalist (Augusta, GA),* December 29, 1869; "Roger A. Pryor," *Milwaukee Daily Sentinel,* March 3, 1865. See also McClean's account in McClean to Roger A. Pryor Jr., May 8, 1889, in *Capture of Gen. Roger A. Pryor,* 7; and *Richmond Daily Dispatch,* March 1, 1865.

89. "Light from Mr. Pryor," *New York Daily Tribune,* March 18, 1889; "Pryor's Political Predictions," *Bridgeton (NJ) Pioneer,* March 29, 1889; "General Pryor on the New South," *Morrisville (VT) News and Citizen,* April 3, 1889.

90. "General Pryor Was Captured," *Manning (SC) Times,* July 17, 1889.

91. *Abbeville (SC) Medium,* quoted in *Watchman and Southron* (Sumter, SC), April 10, 1889; "Is Roger A. Pryor a Deserter?" *Alexandria (VA) Gazette,* April 22, 1889.

92. *Alexandria (VA) Gazette,* April 27, 1889.

93. *Indianapolis Journal,* May 8, 1889.

94. "Gen. Pryor's Statement Denied," *Newberry (SC) Herald and News,* May 9, 1889; "About General Pryor," *Alexandria (VA) Gazette,* May 9, 1889.

95. "A Statement from Gen. Pryor," *Newberry (SC) Herald and News,* April 25, 1889.

96. Wilcox to Roger A. Pryor Jr., May 3, 1889, in *Capture of Gen. Roger A. Pryor,* 1–2.

97. Graduating from Brown University in 1861, Burrage enlisted in the 36th Regiment Massachusetts Volunteer Infantry as a private, rose to the rank of captain, and in June 1864 was wounded at the Battle of Cold Harbor. After recovering from his wounds, Burrage rejoined his unit for most of the Petersburg siege.

98. "The Capture of Roger A. Pryor," *New York Herald,* December 3, 1864, from *Richmond Examiner,* November 30, 1864.

99. Dudley to Pryor Jr., affidavit, April 26, 1889, in *Capture of Gen. Roger A. Pryor,* 2–4.

100. *New York Herald,* quoted in "General Pryor Was Captured," *Manning (SC) Times,* July 17, 1889.

101. Pryor, *Reminiscences*, 173.

102. "'General' Roger A. Pryor Redivivus," *Philadelphia Evening Telegraph*, September 6, 1866.

3. In Search of Reconciliation

1. Quoted in "Greeley in Good Humor," *Arkansas Gazette (Little Rock)*, January 31, 1866.

2. Pryor to *Richmond Whig*, October 5, 1867, in Pryor, *My Day*, 326–29.

3. *Frank Leslie's Illustrated Newspaper*, May 13, 1865.

4. Pryor, *My Day*, 252–57.

5. "Assassination of President Lincoln!," *Richmond Whig*, April 17, 1865.

6. Quoted in *Cadiz (OH) Sentinel*, March 8, 1865.

7. "Sensible at Last," *Cedar Falls (IA) Gazette*, November 22, 1867.

8. "Converted to Sense and Reason," *Daily Oregonian (Portland)*, November 7, 1867.

9. *Lowell (MA) Daily Citizen*, May 16, 1865.

10. "Roger A. Pryor—A Talk with Him," *Cincinnati Gazette*, in *Bel Air (MD) Aegis & Intelligencer*, June 16, 1865.

11. "The Phalanx Forming," *St. Louis Globe-Democrat*, June 23, 1876.

12. See Broomall, *Private Confederacies;* Carmichael, *War for the Common Soldier;* David Silkenat, *Moments of Despair: Suicide, Divorce, and Debt in Civil War Era North Carolina* (Chapel Hill: University of North Carolina Press, 2011); and Diane Miller Sommerville, *Aberration of Mind: Suicide and Suffering in the Civil War–Era South* (Chapel Hill: University of North Carolina Press, 2018).

13. Pryor, *Reminiscences*, 398.

14. *Pittsburgh Daily Commercial*, September 19, 1865.

15. *Potter Journal and News (Coudersport, PA)*, October 3, 1865.

16. Pryor, *Reminiscences*, 398.

17. *Norfolk Virginian*, January 2, 1869. See also William A. Blair, *With Malice toward Some: Treason and Loyalty in the Civil War Era* (Chapel Hill: University of North Carolina Press, 2014).

18. *Alexandria (VA) Gazette*, February 27, 1865.

19. *Howard Union* (Glasgow, MO), November 2, 1865; *Lancaster (PA) Daily Evening Express*, November 14, 1865; *Fort Wayne (IN) Daily Gazette*, November 18, 1865; *Ebensburg (PA) Alleghenian*, November 16, 1865.

20. Pryor, *My Day*, 279.

21. "Letter from New York," *Vermont Watchman (Montpelier)*, October 5, 1866.

22. *San Francisco Daily Evening Bulletin*, July 31, 1865.

23. Pryor, *My Day*, 281–82.

24. Pryor, *My Day*, 282–83.

25. Pryor, *My Day*, 283.

26. Pryor, *My Day*, 284.

27. Pryor, *My Day*, 285.

28. Pryor, *My Day*, 286.

29. Pryor, *My Day*, 292.

30. Daniel E. Sutherland, *The Confederate Carpetbaggers* (Baton Rouge: Louisiana State University Press, 1988), 102.

31. Pryor, *My Day*, 293–95.

32. Roger to Sara, March 5, 1867, in Pryor, *My Day*, 299.

33. Pryor, *My Day*, 300–301.

34. See "The Case of Rev. G. T. Williams," *New York Times*, November 7, 1866; "The Alleged Clerical Pickpocket Case—The Examination Resumed," *Richmond Dispatch*, November 24, 1866; and "Case of Rev. George T. Williams—Retribution," *Louisville Daily Courier*, December 20, 1866.

35. "Ex-Rebels in New York," *San Francisco Evening Bulletin*, March 30, 1869.

36. Pryor, *Reminiscences*, 280, 292–93, 303–15.

37. "Gen. Pryor Rampant," *Georgia Weekly Telegraph and Georgia Journal and Messenger (Macon)*, May 30, 1871.

38. *Norfolk Virginian*, February 3, 1875; Robert Shalen, "The Beecher-Tilton Affair," *New Yorker*, June 4, 1954, https://www.newyorker.com/magazine/1954/06/12/the-beecher-tilton-case-ii.

39. *Daily Critic (Washington, DC)*, November 5, 1875.

40. Pryor, *My Day*, 357; "Beecher-Tilton Echoes," *Leavenworth (KS) Times*, January 9, 1877.

41. "A Roaring Farce," *Milwaukee Daily Sentinel*, January 11, 1875.

42. Quoted in Pryor, *My Day*, 357–58.

43. Quoted in *New Orleans Bulletin*, February 4, 1875. For another description of Pryor during the trial, see "The Beecher Trial," *Milwaukee Daily Sentinel*, February 1, 1875.

44. "Gotham Gossip," *Milwaukee Daily Sentinel*, August 19, 1883.

45. *Kansas City Evening Star*, September 12, 1884.

46. *Chattanooga Daily Times*, October 30, 1887. See also "Gen. Pryor Engaged," *Norfolk Virginian*, September 20, 1887; and "The Anarchist Cases," *Chattanooga Daily Times*, September 25, 1887. For further information, see James R. Green, *Death in the Haymarket: A Story of Chicago, the First Labor Movement, and the Bombing That Divided Gilded Age America* (New York: Pantheon, 2006). For casualties, see ibid., 191–92.

47. *Chattanooga Daily Times*, March 11, 1880; *Georgia Weekly Telegraph (Macon)*, May 7, 1880.

48. *Norfolk Virginian*, September 18, 1885; *Texas Siftings (Austin)*, September 26, 1885; "Gleanings from Gotham," *Galveston Daily News*, January 10, 1886.

49. McSeveney, "Revenge for the Carpetbaggers," 39; Sutherland, *Confederate Carpetbaggers,* 104–5.

50. Pryor, *My Day,* 317.

51. *New York Sun,* August 16, 1884.

52. "O'Donnell's Trial," *St. Louis Globe-Democrat,* October 5, 1883; "Roger A. Pryor: His Connection with the O'Donnell Trial," *Chicago Daily Tribune,* December 22, 1883; "Tynan in Brooklyn," *San Francisco Daily Evening Bulletin,* May 21, 1883; "Roger A. Pryor's Brief," *Galveston Daily News,* December 6, 1883.

53. *New York Tribune,* April 26, 1880.

54. *Jackson (MS) Daily Clarion,* March 30, 1876; Pryor to Butler, n.d., in "The Resignation of Gov. Ames," *St. Louis Globe-Democrat,* April 15, 1876.

55. "Gen. Roger A. Pryor Congratulates Butler," *New York Times,* November 14, 1882.

56. Sutherland, *Confederate Carpetbaggers,* 250–51.

57. "Beecher-Tilton Echoes," *New York Sun,* January 9, 1877.

58. *New York Times,* August 30, 1874; *Brooklyn Sunday Sun,* August 30, 1874; *New Orleans Picayune* quoted in *Winfield (KS) Courier,* December 10, 1874.

59. "Prosperous Pryor," *Milwaukee Journal,* December 13, 1886.

60. "Homes of Southerners," *North American (Philadelphia),* April 17, 1891.

61. McSeveney, "Revenge for the Carpetbaggers," 40.

62. *Chattanooga Dally Times,* February 2, 1885.

63. "An Incident of Cosmopolitan Life," *San Francisco Daily Evening Bulletin,* February 5, 1885.

64. Pryor, *My Day,* 395–96.

65. Pryor, *My Day,* 449.

66. *Proceedings on the Occasion of the Banquet to Celebrate the Seventy-First Anniversary of the Birth of General Ulysses S. Grant* (n.p., 1893), 17–18.

67. "Greeting Grady," *New York Sun,* clippings book, Henry W. Grady Papers, Emory University, Atlanta; William A. Link, *Atlanta, Cradle of the New South: Race and Remembering in the Civil War's Aftermath* (Chapel Hill: University of North Carolina Press, 2013), 138–42.

68. "Future of the Negro," *Brooklyn Daily Eagle,* December 10, 1873.

69. *Vicksburg Herald,* December 19, 1873.

70. "A Jackanape," *Weekly Caucasian (Lexington, MO),* December 20, 1873.

71. "The Negro Problem," *Cincinnati Enquirer,* December 24, 1873.

72. *Chicago Inter Ocean* quoted in "Changes in Ideas in the South," *Alton (IL) Telegraph,* December 26, 1873.

73. "Curious Lecture by Ex-Fire-Eater Roger A. Pryor," *Janesville (WI) Daily Gazette,* December 19, 1873. Pryor's lecture, according to another newspaper, was "a very remarkable proof of the change in feeling toward the negro race which is going on in the minds of all intelligent men." *Weekly Marysville (OH) Tribune,* January 7, 1874.

74. "Colored Democrats," *Milwaukee Journal*, June 5, 1884; "The Colored Democratic Association," *New York Age*, June 14, 1884.

75. *Norfolk Virginian*, October 26, 1875.

76. "An Army Reunion," *Brooklyn Daily Eagle*, October 20, 1875.

77. "Nauseating 'Gush' from a Virginia Fire Eater," *Georgia Weekly Telegraph and Georgia Journal and Messenger (Macon)*, November 2, 1875.

78. David W. Blight, *Race and Reunion: The Civil War in American Memory* (Cambridge, MA: Harvard University Press, 2001), 89–92.

79. *Norfolk Virginian*, April 18, 1877; *New York Tribune*, May 31, 1877.

80. "In Memoriam," *Brooklyn Daily Eagle*, May 25, 1877.

81. The full text of Pryor's speech can be found in *Brooklyn Daily Eagle*, May 31, 1877; *Proceedings on the Evening of Decoration Day, May 30th, 1877, at the Academy of Music, City of Brooklyn, N.Y.* (Brooklyn: Eagle Job and Book Printing, 1877); and "The Soldier, the Friend of Peace and Union," in Pryor, *Essays and Addresses, with Explanatory Notes* (New York: Neale, 1912), 55–82.

82. "The Blue and the Gray," *Junction City (KS) Union*, June 16, 1877.

83. "Twaddle," *Jacksonville (AL) Republican*, June 16, 1877.

84. "The Men Who Caused the War," *Nashville Daily American*, June 8, 1877.

85. *Wilmington (NC) Morning Star*, June 3, 1877.

86. "A Handsome Tribute to a Brooklyn Gentleman," *Utica (NY) Observer*, quoted in *Brooklyn Daily Eagle*, June 5, 1877.

87. "Broadbrim" and "Broadbrim's New York Letter," *Union Springs (AL) Herald and Times*, June 13, 1877.

88. *Savannah Morning News*, March 30, 1889.

89. See, for example, *Norfolk Virginian*, March 23, 1884.

90. *Chattanooga Daily Times*, September 26, 1885.

91. "The General Grant Anniversary," April 27, 1893, in Pryor, *Essays and Addresses*, 85.

92. "Lone Survivor of Sumter Observes War Anniversary," *Washington Times*, April 12, 1911.

93. "But One Survivor of Fort Sumter," *Prescott (AR) Daily News*, April 13, 1911.

94. "Remarks That Puzzled a City," *Caldwell (SC) Watchman*, August 11, 1911.

95. *Charleston News & Courier* quoted in *Richmond Times-Dispatch*, June 11, 1911.

96. "Henry George's Canvass a Feature," *New Orleans Daily Picayune*, October 24, 1897; "Barter of Bosses," *Bismarck (Dak. Terr.) Tribune*, October 29, 1897.

97. "Gen. Roger A. Pryor Dies in 91st Year," *New York Times*, March 15, 1919.

98. "Death of Mrs. Roger A. Pryor," *Washington Post*, February 17, 1912; "Roger A. Pryor Goes into the Great Unknown," *Atlanta Constitution*, March 15, 1919.

INDEX